Economic Citizens

Economic Citizens

A Narrative of Asian American Visibility

Christine So

TEMPLE UNIVERSITY PRESS
Philadelphia

TEMPLE UNIVERSITY PRESS
1601 North Broad Street
Philadelphia PA 19122
www.temple.edu/tempress

Published 2007

Printed in the United States of America

♾ The paper used in this publication meets the requirements of the American National Standard for Information Sciences—Permanence of Paper for Printed Library Materials, ANSI Z39.48-1992

Library of Congress Cataloging-in-Publication Data
So, Christine, 1967–
Economic citizens : a narrative of Asian American visibility / Christine So.
p. cm.
Includes bibliographical references and index.
ISBN-13: 978-1-59213-584-4 ISBN-10: 1-59213-584-6 (cloth : alk. paper)
1. Asian Americans—Economic conditions. 2. Exchange—United States. 3. Social exchange. 4. Globalization—Social aspects—United States. 5. Asian Americans—Ethnic identity. 6. Asian Americans—Historiography. 7. Asian Americans in literature. 8. United States—Ethnic relations. I. Title.
E184.A75S66 2007
305.895′1073001—dc22

2007006357

2 4 6 8 9 7 5 3 1

For my mother
Sofia C. So
and
in memory of my father,
Antero G. So
(1932–2007)

Contents

Acknowledgments

This book was greatly improved by the input of colleagues and friends who contributed significantly to each phase of the book's development. In particular Kandice Chuh first envisioned how the manuscript might be restructured into a more coherent narrative. Her careful and critically astute reading of the entire manuscript enabled me to make substantial improvements. Lucy Maddox and Sarita See read multiple drafts with tremendous speed and brilliance; they are my heroes. And Lori Merish's comments towards the end of the process helped me to shape the book into its final form. Throughout the book's evolution, they all encouraged its progress and my own scholarly development, and I am very fortunate to have them as mentors and friends.

Certainly the book would not have existed without the early and sustained efforts of Sau-ling C. Wong, whose guidance has been crucial to my career as an Asian Americanist and whose extensive body of work has indelibly shaped my own critical vision. Despite heavy demands on their time and energy, Sau-ling Wong and Elaine H. Kim provided for me a foundation in Asian American literary studies. I have deeply appreciated their encouragement for many years. Also central to my work has been the community that Juliana

Chang and Karen Su have afforded me; I am thankful for their friendship and expertise.

I am indebted to Janet Francendese for her support of this project. She and her colleagues' professionalism has made every stage of this book's publication a pleasure. Thanks are especially owed to her and Temple University Press for their long commitment to publishing in the field of Asian American studies.

Georgetown University and its English department assisted in the writing of this book with summer grants and a junior faculty sabbatical. Many members (former and current) of my department have also played a role in the book's sculpting and refining. I am especially grateful to Pam Fox for her mentorship and her insightful comments on the book. Kim Hall and Michael Ragussis have made these past years richer with their humor, perceptiveness, and smart advice. Conversations about my work with Matthew Tinkcom, Anne Cubilié, and Lalitha Gopalan have consistently led me to fertile intellectual ground. I also thank (former and current) department chairs Leona Fisher, Joseph Sitterson, and Penn Szittya for their efforts to support my and other junior faculty members' research and professional development.

My family has always made it easier for me to do my work. I thank my parents, Sofia C. and Antero G. So, and my sister, Mary June So, for their limitless faith and sustenance. Norma and Phil Gomez provided many good wishes and an equal number of hours of babysitting. And finally, my deepest gratitude goes to Zoë Gomez-So for the extraordinary joy she brings to my life, and especially to Phillip Gomez, III, for the last twenty-one years.

Introduction

> Counting money had become almost a hobby to [Wang Chi-yang], and he enjoyed it as much as he did attending his miniature garden. After he had counted the total sum, he sorted the bills according to their denominations, then sorted them once more according to their degree of newness, putting the brand-new ones on one pile, the newer ones on another and the old ones on a third. . . . He would spend the old ones first and the new ones later; as for the brand-new ones, he would save them in an exquisitely carved sandalwood box locked in one of his desk drawers.
>
> —C. Y. Lee, The *Flower Drum Song*

This passage, published in 1957, depicts an extraordinary moment of Chinese American alienation. Wang Chi-yang, representative of first generation Chinese American immigrants in the novel, sorts his money alone. What is striking about the passage is neither his careful counting of bills nor the copious amounts of currency. Instead, we realize what is odd about the scene is his alternative valuation of money—not according to what the bills might purchase, but in terms of their "newness," their time of entry into economic circulation. Wang Chi-yang's removal of money from circulation parallels his own isolation in San Francisco's Chinatown. Depicted as an old-fashioned relic from a pre-Communist, Confucist society, he wears long gowns, employs obedient servants, and expects filial piety from his sons. He also hoards most of his considerable fortune in a large trunk in his home. Impervious to pleas from his family to deposit the money in a bank, Wang Chi-yang instead converts a one-hundred-dollar bill each week into smaller denominations and stacks, categorizes, and organizes the various denominations, like a collector with prized artifacts.

Money, however, as George Simmel reminds us, stands as the symbolic marker for the exchange of objects; money in essence represents exchange. He explains, "Money has acquired the value it possesses as a means of exchange; if there is nothing to exchange, money has no value. . . . Money has no place where there is no mutual relationship, either because one does not want anything from other people, or because one lives on a different plane—without any relation to them as it were—and is able to satisfy any need without any service in return" (156). Money then becomes a means of marking Wang Chi-yang's outsider status, his existence "on a different plane," one defined by Chinese artifacts and ancient customs. His use of money—one that denies its role as a symbol of exchange, even as his fetishism of it impossibly imbues it with value outside of exchange—only reinforces his foreignness, his alienation from not only the larger economic structures that surround him, but the social ones as well. As Wang Chi-yang strolls down Grant Avenue and across Bush Street, the borders of San Francisco's Chinatown seem to mark not only the essence of "Chineseness" but also the boundaries of an alternative economic realm. From this perspective, there is no "mutual relationship" between Chinatown and a non-Chinese America.

And yet, as Pardee Lowe notes in describing his father's business expansion in his 1943 memoir, *Father and Glorious Descendant*, "A new economic activity was born" (8). Written less than a decade apart, set in Chinatown and equally reflective of the anxieties of Chinese Americanization, *Father and Glorious Descendant* and *The Flower Drum Song* also share a surprisingly disproportionate focus on the circulation and exchange of commodities. Replete with images of money, commodities, buying, lending, banking, and selling, these narratives and others from this era, ones that have traditionally been dismissed because of their exoticizing of Chinatown and Chinese culture, ultimately belie their assimilationist rhetoric. They instead demonstrate that despite the promise of economic exchange as a means toward social integration, Asian Americans are in the end unable to escape the economic circuits that keep them as tightly contained as Chinatown's boundaries.

Questions over money determine the narrative trajectory of a number of Asian American texts published in the last fifty years—what money can buy, how money is lost, how money is circulated, and what labor or objects are worth. Works such as Pardee Lowe's *Father and Glorious Descendant* (1943), Jade Snow Wong's *Fifth Chinese Daughter* (1950), C. Y. Lee's *The Flower Drum Song* (1957), Virginia Chin-lan Lee's *The House that Tai Ming Built* (1963), Wanwadee Larsen's *Confessions of a Mail Order Bride* (1989), David Mura's *Turning Japanese: Memoirs of a Sansei* (1991), Lydia Minatoya's *Talking To High Monks in the Snow* (1992), Pang-Mei Natasha Chang's *Bound Feet and Western Dress* (1996), Adeline Yen Mah's *Falling Leaves: The Story of an Unwanted Chinese Daughter* (1998), and Winberg and May-lee Chai's *The Girl From Purple Mountain* (2001)—works I examine in *Economic Citizens*—have been primarily read as narratives of alienation, assimilation, and the assertion of ethnic and gendered identities. I argue instead that it is actually the narratives of economic circulation that make the paradoxical nature of those other processes fully visible. It is through the language of economic exchange, in fact, that we can locate underlying anxieties about the relationship between Asian Americans and the larger American nation, and recurring doubts over the ability to convert difference into sameness, disenfranchisement into universality, the racial minority into the abstract citizen.

Economic exchange offers an illusory means of entering into these larger communities. Not only does a belief in money signify a communal agreement over the value of a piece of paper or coin (an object that has no value beyond that agreement), but the act of exchange itself at the very least signals an albeit brief relationship between two parties. In speaking of the relationship between agents of exchange, Karl Marx argues, "Each of the subjects is an exchanger, i.e. each has the same social relation towards the other that the other has towards him. As subjects of exchange, their relation is therefore that of equality. It is impossible to find any trace of distinction, not to speak of contradiction, between them; not even a difference" (*Capital*, 241). Of course Marx's point is that they are not truly "equal"; the contradiction of capital, however, necessitates that that exchange be based on equality, a presumption that in fact disguises the unequal class relations that exist.

As other critics have noted, however, Marx's theory fails to account for the ways that race impacts and further intensifies the contradictions of capital. These texts—largely written for mainstream audiences—vividly reveal the contradictory effects of race not only on the production of capital but also on economic exchange in general. And, in fact, we find in these works that the anxiety surrounding economic equivalence and the faith in Americanization, universality, and the transcendence of their racialized bodies is marked by a "hyper-Asianness"—an elaborate conjuring of Chinese customs, Japanese roots, or Thai culture. In these works, written for mainstream audiences and often published by major publishing houses, one's essential Asian heritage is presented as an exotic and yet easily digestible experience. Although it is not surprising that these texts use readers' assumptions about the alien and alienated Asian as a means of celebrating a universality of struggle and beliefs, I would argue that a closer examination of this process is needed beyond condemning the consumption of these works. We see in these critically ignored or dismissed narratives the complex and paradoxical nature of visibility and the possibilities for how we might read the recent appearances of Asian Americans within the larger public sphere. Beyond the identification of stereotypes that proliferate within the texts, this project instead bears witness to how the racial surplus of the Asian body works against, negotiates, and capitulates to its own expansion.

Mapping race along the axis of economic exchange enables the articulation of a striking narrative of Asian American identity formation—one that demonstrates the power and ubiquitousness of the economic realm as a means of bringing people into relation with one another, and one that maps the strict and confining limits of economic circulation for racialized Americans as a pathway into abstract citizenship. Asian Americans have overwhelmingly been imagined through the rhetoric and logic of economics, defined as agents of vast economic profit or loss. Economic exchange, however, is supposed to function as a fixed, contained, and stable relationship in which goods are traded for other goods with equal value. The very premise of economic transacting depends on a "homogenous field of goods"; that is, every object and person must stand in calculable relation to every other object and person.[1] Furthermore, such a system functions on the assumption that such exchanges are transparent and are enacted between fully formed subjects. Authors such as C. Y. Lee, Jade Snow Wong, Lydia Minatoya, and Adeline Mah demonstrate, however, the endless work that is needed to make these equations, to calculate and manage and negotiate the terms and rates of exchange. Ultimately these texts, which themselves are highly commodifiable, call into question the logic of these exchanges, while unveiling the unstable and unclear terms of their actualization. We discover that economic exchange both produces and reflects the fluid and fraught nature of racialized identity construction.[2]

It seems crucial in this era—defined almost overwhelmingly by economic exchange—that we consider how such transactions determine Asian American subjectivities and in turn how race rewrites such exchanges. Such a paradigm enables us to see that the other conditions and oppositions that we have historically used to theorize Asian Americans' position vis-à-vis the U.S. nation-state—inclusion/exclusion, invisibility/visibility, silence/voice, alienation/assimilation—are in fact not as clearly divisible or opposed as we might have originally imagined. What I am arguing here is that visible, or even seemingly wholesale, entry into the state's apparatuses and its institutions and corporations does not necessarily mean that racial difference has been contained, co-opted, and managed. Instead we see in these texts an anxiety that permeates all exchanges between margin and mainstream—the presence of a racial excess that can neither be specifically quantified, exactly accounted for, nor fully erased.

Such a project—one that looks more closely at how Asian Americans enter and appropriate U.S. mainstream culture and ideologies—seemingly moves against the grain of current critical work in Asian American Studies. Originally grounded in a nation-based battle for community empowerment, Asian Americanists have in the last decade seriously interrogated both their foundational definitions of *community* and the field's reliance on nation-based models of identity and empowerment. Critics have instead demonstrated that analyses and conceptualizations of "Asian America" cannot be located solely within the borders of the United States. Not only do such earlier theories fail to take account of the pressures of globalization and the recent decline of the nation-state's centrality, but they also elide the complex relations between the United States and Asia that have determined U.S. policies toward and cultural constructions of Asians in the United States.[3] Critics have thus argued that Asian Americanists' efforts to "claim America" and to achieve inclusion into the larger national body necessitate a corresponding acknowledgment of the United States' imperial history in Asia (see Chuh and Shimakawa, *Orientations*, 278). And finally, while the field's political grounding in the United States has previously depended on a necessary distancing from all things Asian, recent scholarship has instead reoriented the field *toward* Asia and the Asian diaspora.

The object of *community* has undergone equally important scrutiny. If external relationships among Asian America, the United States, and Asia have been theoretically remapped, boundaries within the Asian American community have also been redrawn. Defined by a diverse group of Asian ethnicities—which themselves have complex political, economic, and social relationships within Asian American Studies as well as within the larger national and global arenas—earlier evocations of an Asian American community have become significantly destabilized. Critics have also demonstrated that the establishment of an Asian American subjectivity revolved initially around masculine and heterosexual norms. At the same time, the increased institutionalization of Asian American Studies and Ethnic Studies at elite institutions even as conditions for racial minorities have worsened, seems to suggest that the field and its original goal of radical Asian American community empowerment have only been partially successful.[4] And finally, critics have begun to deconstruct what have been, up until now, basic and universal assumptions about the coherence of the Asian American subject and the disciplinary fields within which he has been traditionally studied. Kandice Chuh and Laura Hyun-Yi Kang, respectively, have instead called for a "subjectless" discourse and an interdisciplinary means of reading and theorizing Asian American culture and politics. Asian American Studies' fragmentation and reformulation have coincided with an emphasis on hybridity and heterogeneity (Lowe) and more multiethnic and interracial approaches to reading an Asian American history and present (Song and James Lee). King Kok Cheung summarizes the recent developments as follows: We have moved "from seeking to 'claim America' to forging a connection between Asia and Asian America; from centering on race and on masculinity to revolving around the multiple axes of ethnicity, gender, class, and sexuality; from being concerned primarily with social and communal responsibility to being caught in the quandaries and possibilities of postmodernism and multiculturalism" (quoted in Ty and Goellnicht, 1).

Such reconceptualizations of Asian American Studies and of Asian America have been necessary and path breaking not only for critics in our own field but also for theorists of American Studies and critical race and ethnicity studies. While much of the recent scholarship has focused on reimagining, resituating, and deconstructing definitions of Asian American identity as well as on mapping the constantly shifting and contested grounds on which that identity currently maneuvers (whether across continents, ethnicities, histories, disciplines, methodologies, or epistemologies), this project instead takes as its focus a conceptualization of Asian America as it is more concretely, wholly, universally, and even stereotypically constructed. Although I fully support—and hope this book contributes to—Asian American Studies critics' efforts to resist dominant ideologies and imperialist histories, to dissect carefully our own critical methodologies, and to imagine new ways of practicing Asian American Studies, I would argue that is equally important—especially in this era of global capitalism, mass commodification and consumerism, and widespread co-optation and institutionalization of all forms of resistance—to explore more fully Asian American culture's production of not only difference but sameness, nativization, assimilation, and belonging. Such a project does not ignore or discount the history of racialization, exclusion, and alienation of Asians in the United States—on the contrary—instead, it charts more fully how Asian Americans make an appearance in the American imaginary. Far from being an easy process of reiteration and mimicry, such moments of assimilation actually make visible the impossibility of abstract citizenship. Through the lens of economic exchange, a system that brings all people and objects in relation to one another, we see not only the promise and limits of economic activity as a means of achieving social relations, but also the anxiety and slippages inherent in the production, circulation, and translation of Asian Americanness. In these texts, in other words, texts that repeatedly assert sameness and universality, we are made acutely aware that such declarations of belonging ultimately are only one moment in a chain of Sisyphean efforts to make incomprehensible and incomparable social, economic, and symbolic equations add up.

This project thus engages with the notion of economic exchange in three primary contexts. First, Asians and Asian Americans have been represented historically and even more so in the current era as agents of capitalism gone awry. In other words, it is the possibility of Asia's economic expansion (more often characterized as domination) and the specter of billions of Asian buyers, laborers, and sellers that has most often recently characterized Asians' (and by extension Asian Americans') appearance in American culture. Second, the economic sphere has been and continues to be directly linked, as Jurgen Habermas explains, to the rise and subsequent decline of the public sphere. Any analysis of how Asian Americans are imagined and negotiate their own position in U.S. culture and society necessitates a clearer sense of how their role as the conduit—or alternately the threat—to U.S. economic wealth informs their own cultural constructions. Conversely, Asian American culture offers a means for a clearer understanding of how the economic and social spheres function in tandem with one another especially with respect to racialized bodies. Although economic activity has been generally regarded as a means toward or substitute for social participation—a history I discuss in greater detail shortly—we see in the texts I name above an ongoing anxiety over the pathways of economic and social circulation. For far from being a steady and reliable means of abstraction in which Asian Americans might stand as an undifferentiated node in the circuits of economic exchange or as disembodied national citizens, these routes of economic and social circulation paradoxically only ensure the reverse—the hyperembodied racialized subject.

Third, this project implicitly addresses the underlying question of how we as critics might "value" Asian American literature, given the twin impulses in recent years toward on the one hand, the institutionalization and commercialization of race and race studies, and on the other hand, the deconstruction of all forms of value and value-making. As Asian Americanists like Kandice Chuh have moved boldly toward "subjectlessness," (see Kandice Chuh, *Imagine Otherwise*) the hypervisible, commodified, assimilated, and excessive Asian stands in extreme at the opposite end of this trajectory for how critics might imagine the Asian American as functioning within the U.S. cultural imaginary. The narratives and structures of economic exchange offer a critical means for mapping these presumably normalizing circuits across a range of local, national, and transnational spaces, spaces in which the Asian American's various metamorphoses—her disembodiment or hyperembodiment—ultimately disrupt and render extraordinary these basic routes of circulation.

U.S. Capital Formation and the Specter of Asian Americans

Historically, Asians have been defined in the United States as exceeding the acceptable limits of capital.[5] They earn too much money (in the United States), they earn too little money (in Asia), they work too much (China and India), consume too few American products (China) or too many American properties (Japan), and in short represent the United States' greatest economic threat and opportunity. In the nineteenth century, Asians in the United States were rendered symbolic of the overexploitation of labor, while at the beginning of the twentieth century, the embodied the seduction of consumption. By the century's end, they were representative of upward mobility and the expansion of multinational capital. While Asian American critics have demonstrated that Asians have historically been utilized to reinforce national ideologies regarding whiteness, class, gender, and sexuality, I particularly highlight here that it has been the logic of capital and the threat that Asians present that has enabled the consolidation of the white, middle-class family identity.

In the late nineteenth century, the "coolie" was defined as "unfree" and "servile," a designation of exploited and exploitable labor against which a white working class could be created (Robert Lee, 61). In March of 1876, the *Marin Journal* offered a resolution against Chinese residents in California, the first of which reads, "*That* he is a slave, reduced to the lowest terms of beggarly economic, and is no fit competitor for an American freeman" (Robert Lee, 62). Although the "coolie" threatens the white laborer in that his labor value can be purchased for less money, what I find striking about this quotation is that the *Marin Journal* asserts that the problem of the Chinese in California is precisely that he is "no fit competitor," in other words, that he does not function as a *suitable* threat. The resolution instead, in an effort to expel Chinese peoples from California, imagines a community whereby one's unsuitability to circulate economically becomes the prohibiting factor for social inclusion.

Throughout the twentieth century, "the lowest terms of beggarly economic" are transformed into threats of economic excess. In his analysis of Cecil B. De Mille's *The Cheat* (1915), Robert Lee links the character of the Japanese merchant (named "Tori" and played by Sessue Hayakawa) to the dangers of overconsumption for the new middle-class white woman at the turn of the century.[6] The popularity of "oriental" art and commodities during this time combines with anxieties over Japan's dominance in Asia and U.S. imperialism in the Philippines, Guam, and Hawaii to once again locate the Oriental outside social and familial norms by casting him as the agent and object of excess desire and addiction, one that dangerously tempts the middle-class white woman from traditional duties within the family. Lee writes, "At a moment in which the reproduction of the national family is threatened by bourgeois over-civilization, Tori represents both the seductiveness of Oriental luxury and the danger of over-consumption" (124).

In the second half of the twentieth century, we can once again see the evocation of Asians as representations of capital that has overrun its boundaries. The explicit articulation of Japanese Americans and Chinese Americans as model minorities in 1966 provided a counterpoint to anxieties and rationalizations of economically disenfranchised African Americans and confirmed the continued propagation of the American dream. If one hundred years previously, Asians were deemed "no fit competitor," they now were imagined as hyperfit, predetermined by "Confucist" and other inherent cultural values to achieve economic success. In his analysis of William Petersen's "Success Story, Japanese American style," widely acknowledged as the inception of the "model-minority myth," David Palumbo-Liu points to the link Petersen makes between Japanese Americans' "phenomenal economic and social success" and Japan's ability to modernize. If Asian Americans previously embodied the economic threat that served to consolidate the white working class and then later to remind white middle-class women of the dangers of overconsumption, they now modeled economic overachievement and adaptability, whether to America or to modernity in general. The very nature of their excess, however, would once again render them alien to the American body (*Asian/American*, 179).

Certainly in the last quarter of a century, we have witnessed the full-blown identification of Asia with capital. In the eighties, media attention and books focused on the rapid economic growth in Japan, Singapore, South Korea, Taiwan, and Hong Kong, and more recently, anxiety has crystallized around the economic rise of China and India. Robert G. Lee notes the emergence of a racial discourse that constructed Asian Americans as agents of Orientalized capital. "In this construction of the Oriental, it is not only the Asian American who is Orientalized; multinational capital itself is imbued with oriental cultural difference" (205). The threat of Asian economic dominance was particularly made manifest in a 1987 *Time Magazine* article entitled "For Sale: America." The epigraph reads:

> "Everything here is so cheap."
>
> —a Japanese real estate agent visiting Manhattan

In the article Stephen Koepp sounds the alarm: that foreigners—Japanese, British, Canadian, South Korean, West German, and Swiss peoples and companies—are buying corporations and brands like Doubleday, Brooks Brothers, Smith and Wesson, Carnation Foods, and General Tires; and prime urban real estate in Manhattan, Los Angeles, the District of Columbia, and acres of forests in Washington and Oregon, mines in Montana and Nevada, and vineyards in Northern California. Although Koepp is careful not to single out the Japanese as the only foreign investors, his language about them echoes the predominant rhetoric characterizing Japan during that time—that their unidimensional appetite for investment is voraciously and indiscriminately consuming the multifaceted history and culture of the United States, its Manhattan skyline, Las Vegas casinos, heartland factories, and Hawaiian resorts. Koepp writes, "Japan, the world's largest creditor country . . . has the mightiest bankroll of all to engage in buying America," and quotes a director of McKinsey consulting firm, "In the next two or three years, Japanese investments here will build up very rapidly. It's going to become a torrent."

Fears of a torrent of Japanese imports and investments were also heightened during the eighties by claims of Japan's homogeneity and alien culture. Unlike British or Canadian investments, Japan's purchasing of U.S. companies and real estate was imagined as both an economic and cultural invasion, an assault that coincided with the changing demographics of the United States. The influx of Latino and Asian immigrants and of Asian investments, combined with a downturn in the U.S. economy, led to a violent reconsolidation of "American" from calls to "Buy American" to the televised destruction of Japanese products, to actual violence against Asian Americans.[7]

The threat of Asian capital and Asians *as* capital seems to have morphed in the last decade into an overall anxiety about global capital in general.[8] With special attention to China and India, we have seen recent media reports that have highlighted the outsourcing of jobs, the influx of imports, and the consumption of Asian culture, and the rising economic growth of the world's two most populous countries has raised questions about how the United States is poised to meet the challenges of the twenty-first century. Recently, *Newsweek* announced a series of reports on China, the first featuring actress Ziyi Zhang on its cover and announcing, "China's Century" (May 9, 2005). In it, editor Mark Whitaker writes, "There's no question that China's astounding growth, vast and industrious population and rapid embrace of new technology and education have put it on a glide path to challenging U.S. pre-eminence" (6).

Unlike previous constructions of Japan as economic threat and enemy, the implication now is that China represents a global economic future, one that Americans need to meet fully. Correspondingly, the issue includes articles about American high school students who astutely take Chinese language classes, or alternately, local tensions in China surrounding preparations for the Olympics (to be held in Beijing in 2008), and columns entitled, "What America Needs To Do." Fareed Zakeria advises:

> The answer for Western countries cannot be to shut themselves off from this new reality. After all, they benefit from the expansion of global commerce. . . . [C]ountries that have tried to wall themselves off from the rest of the world in the past—to maintain their economy or culture—have stagnated. Those that have embraced change have flourished. China is simply the biggest part of a new world. You cannot switch it off. (39)

Economic engagement with China seems imperative and also extremely daunting. What threatens us, however, is not only that we will lose the battle for global economic preeminence, but also that we will be overwhelmed by Asians and by economic activity and excess itself. Asians have historically symbolized economic imbalance, an association that reveals certainly that racialized identities are constructed through the machine of capital but also that economics itself is racialized.

Economic Citizenship and the Public Sphere

The now-ubiquitous representations of Asians' and Asian Americans' robot-like and hypercompetitive natures serve to emphasize their foreignness, their inability to achieve the humanity necessary for full Americanization. Aihwa Ong notes the efforts of Chinese diaspora members in the United States to shift from economic to social participation. She writes, "Chinese developers who live in San Francisco are trying harder to erase the image of themselves as 'economic animals' who build monster houses, as well as the perception that they lack a sense of civic duty and responsibility" (*Flexible Citizenship*, 103). The leap from the economic to the social, however, can be more complex than the developers imagine, as economic exchange is open to outsiders in ways that social circulation is not. George Simmel explains that it is precisely because of their exclusion from an established community that the alienated have historically turned to economic trade. Speaking specifically of the Jewish diaspora, he writes, "Dispersed peoples, crowded into more or less closed cultural circles, can hardly put down roots or find a free position in production. They are therefore dependent on intermediate trade which is much more elastic than primary production, since the sphere of trade can be expanded almost limitlessly by merely formal combinations and can absorb people from outside whose roots do not lie in the group" (225). Despite economic exchange's capacity for absorption, the role of money as a stimulus for social acceptance has historically been a subject for debate. Early philosophers such as Aristotle and Thomas Aquinas criticized any exchange that occurred beyond that needed for sustenance and self-sufficiency. Exchange for the accumulation of money or profit, in other words, was considered "contrary to nature" and created an imbalance in the relations between households (Parry and Bloch, 2).

Money as the means for a community's expansion or alternately its breakdown has historically functioned as a central theme in debates surrounding the societal benefits of economic exchange. Critics Karl Marx and George Simmel, for example, differ in their assessments of the effects of economic exchange (ibid., 4). Marx argues that market exchange not only alienates the laborer from his product but also isolates members of the community from each other. Money, in effect, adversely affects communal identity. Simmel, on the other hand, sees economic exchange as a means of widening existing social circles and transferring an adherence to one's community to a larger dependence on an abstract system of exchange (ibid., 4–5). Maurice Bloch and Jonathan Parry explain, "The impersonality and anonymity of money, it is argued, lends itself to the impersonal and inconsequential relationships characteristic of the market-place and even to a complete anonymity in exchange. Destructive of community, money depersonalizes social relations" (6). The "depersonalization of social relations," as I demonstrate in the following chapters, presents both opportunities and obstacles. Even as economic exchange enables the inclusion of Asians into a more largely defined community, Asian Americans resist and attempt to transcend their largely impersonal and anonymous roles in those exchanges. We see throughout these works the hyperestablishment of identity, the almost frantic effort to first, emphasize distinctive characteristics and meaningful moments of social contact, and second, abstract those differences into a narrative of national and humanistic belonging.

Despite these critiques of money's impact on nuclear communities, Charles Taylor demonstrates that in the development of Western modernity, economic relationships of production, exchange, and consumption came to be seen as the dominant theory of how society best operates. Moving away from premodern notions of warfare, society began to believe in economic security and prosperity as the ideal means of achieving the greater common good and a more "civilized" existence. Taylor writes, "Conceiving of the economy as a system is an achievement of eighteenth-century theorists . . . but coming to see the most important purpose and agenda of society as economic collaboration and exchange is a drift in our social imaginary, which begins in that period and continues to this day" (105).

The expansion of circles of economic exchange in fact directly enables, as Jurgen Habermas demonstrates, the creation of the public sphere. Habermas explains that as early as the thirteenth century in Europe, economic trade began to signal a new social structure that existed outside of the strictly contained feudal hierarchies. Through such gatherings as trade fairs and organizations, long-distance trade allowed for new relationships and "dependencies" to extend beyond (without initially threatening) the traditional estate system. By the sixteenth century, however, the mercantile network had as its goal the expansion of capital rather than just subsistence, and their more aggressive efforts to enter new territories and markets subsequently prompted the beginnings of the nation-state and its clearer delineation of its economic, political, and military borders. Capitalism abroad also affected the operation of the domestic economy, as the market and the state imposed new means of taxation to fund these expeditions and new regulations for production—structures necessary for meeting the demands of consumption. The number and range of news outlets also expanded during this time, and the news became a commodity in its own right, seeking a wider readership beyond agents of the marketplace. And the wider circulation and definition of *the news* in turn created an audience that the state could identify and address (14–25). We see here that the expansion of economic trade opened routes of social and cultural circulation and contributed to the creation of the nation-state. The economic constitutes a means for community, a possibility that constitutes the conundrum of many contemporary Asian American texts.

By the late nineteenth century, however, the public sphere began to decline, as issues that had traditionally been debated and resolved in the public arena moved under state control and the private arena was transformed into a space for consumption. Free trade became more constrained as capital and power concentrated among fewer participants; and that imbalance and the desire to protect national economic interests prompted the state toward increased controls and influence over economic trade both nationally and internationally. The media also made a parallel shift from the world of public rational debate to that of commodification and consumption. Here Habermas is particularly critical of the media's tendency to render its material "ready-made convenience, patterned, and predigested" (169), and to present it in a way that discourages response, disagreement, and debate.

Even as Habermas charts the decline of the public sphere, however, critics have raised questions about his theories, debating the existence of rational public debate, interrogating the inclusive nature of the public sphere, questioning his historical contextualization, and asking whether his pronouncements against mass media and culture have been overly pessimistic. Nancy Fraser in particular has argued that the bourgeois public sphere worked in fact to institute new economic hierarchies.[9] I primarily invoke Habermas' work, however, as a means of pointing to the dominant narratives operating in these mainstream Asian American texts. We see there a similar opportunity for economic trade to break down fixed hierarchies, and the effort by Asian American bourgeois classes to transform their economic participation into civic responsibility. We also are witness to the state's interest in expanding economic trade while preserving national interests, and Asian Americans' struggles to narrate their own economic and social circulation given the state's imperative. And finally we see that Asian Americans are ultimately unable to escape the commodification of their own stories even as all of these texts testify to the unreliability of the economic realm as a means of locating their identities. These works, in fact, question the notion that equivalence in economic exchange is achievable, much less sustainable, belying those who have argued that mutual economic benefit constitutes the ideal social state.

The relationship between the economic and racial (and other forms of) identities and subjectivities are further elaborated on when we consider how the circulation and consumption of commodities can reproduce and reiterate hegemonic structures and discourses of race. Arjun Appadurai argues that the circulation of objects is itself defined by and defines contestations of power within communities. He writes:

> It is in the interests of those in power to completely freeze the flow of commodities, by creating a closed universe of commodities and a rigid set of regulations about how they are to move. Yet the very nature of contests between those in power (or those who aspire to greater power) tends to invite a loosening of these rules and an expansion of the pool of commodities. This aspect of elite politics is generally the Trojan horse of value shifts. ("Introduction" to *The Social Life of Things*, 57)

Circulation is thus described here not as a closed system in which value is uniformly and permanently agreed upon, but one which is instead destabilized, subject to the inevitable entry of new commodities and interests. Appadurai's conclusions also make clear that a means of gaining power is through entry into the circulation of commodities, a strategy that I demonstrate in subsequent chapters has been deployed repeatedly by and within Asian American texts, with mixed results. In understanding the circulation of commodities as connected to and, in fact, inseparable from contestations of power, Appadurai provides for us a means of reading the circulation of Asian American objects, identities, and texts as already meeting immediate resistance upon entry into the flow of commodities. What might seem to be the smooth exchange of commodities instead conceals the disruptions that characterize that movement, disruptions that we might read as the traces of racial difference.

Critics in race studies have long been ambivalent about economic exchange as a means for social advancement, and theorists have generally approached the intersection of race, culture, and economics through either Marxist analyses or critiques of the consumption of minority cultures. Both investigations reveal that capital has almost exclusively functioned to exploit and disenfranchise peoples of color. I agree with these arguments and simultaneously raise questions about how to read texts that benefit from capitalism and commodification. It is not surprising, for example, that most of the texts I study focus on middle and upper class Asians and Asian Americans, those who have profited by economic exchange and who subscribe faithfully to the system as a means of well-being and prosperity. I suggest that beyond concluding that these texts are exploitative and co-opted, we might also read them as a means of further comprehending how Asian Americans and other racial minorities are made visible and function in the national public sphere. Critic bell hooks contends that such visibility is ultimately destructive of peoples of color, that consumption of racial otherness only succeeds in erasing difference altogether. Reflective of the predominant scholarship on the consumption of minority cultures, she argues that such consumption provides disaffected whites a means of experiencing the exotic, dangerous, and out of the ordinary, even as those experiences serve to confirm fairly ordinary, persistent. and often imperialist fantasies of the "primitive" Other. Even as she regrets that such consumption can often be seductive to those who are being consumed, because such acts offer "the promise of recognition and reconciliation" (347), she leaves no doubts that "consumption" of racial otherness is nothing short of the wholesale erasure of that racial other's history and subjectivity.[10]

At the same time, others have argued that it is only through consumption and economic exchange that peoples of color can achieve social empowerment. If Asian Americans have been represented largely as the machines of economic exchange, African Americans, as Regina Austin explains, have generally been perceived as alien to economic circulation. Austin begins her essay by arguing

> In so very many areas of public life, blacks are condemned and negatively stereotyped for engaging in activities that white people undertake without a second thought. Among the most significant of these is buying and selling goods and services. Despite the passage of state and federal antidiscrimination and public accommodations laws, blacks are still fighting for the right to shop and the right, if not the reason, to sell. (229)

For Austin, economic empowerment—which is not defined primarily by class status but more by the assertion and acceptance of African Americans' performance as producers, exchangers, and consumers—is narrated through the language of "rights." Unlike Habermas, Austin defines the public sphere as encompassing the marketplace. Such a collapse of the economic and social realms not only demonstrates how economic exchange situates racial minorities in a larger national community but also raises questions about whether stronger economic participation in fact leads to ascendancy in the public sphere. For Austin, greater economic circulation within the black community raises the community as a whole. The narratives I examine in *Economic Citizens*, however, complicate significantly these assumptions. While the writers share Austin's assumptions about the translation of economic rights into civil rights, the paths of economic circulation that they trace rarely run smoothly. Instead, their anxiety about economic exchange opens anew questions of the viability of abstract citizenship for U.S. racial minorities.[11]

The Economic and Literary Criticism

The question of how the economic and the literary function together has lately been the focus of a number of critical investigations, and this project both contributes to and offers new challenges to that body of scholarship. The field of economic criticism as a whole is committed to several fundamental approaches. As the editors of *The New Economic Criticism* summarize, economic critics might assume an "extratextual" approach, one that analyzes the economic context surrounding the production of a literary work, the economic or class status of the author, the author's attitudes toward money or the marketplaces that sell her work. Another methodology concentrates on the "intratextual," the analysis of the metaphors of monetary exchange within a text itself. "When applied to narrative works, such criticism usually begins by analyzing the actions and interactions of the characters—their exchanges, debts, purchases, losses, gifts, etc.—to show how they embody this internal tropic economy" (Osteen and Woodmanse, 36).[12] Economic critics might also question the economy of literature and literary value, that is, questions of canonization, consumption, or aesthetic value. And, finally, economic critics might consider and theorize the practice of economic criticism itself. In short, economic criticism encompasses a wide field of investigation; it has analyzed the simultaneous rise in the eighteenth century of the novel and the science of political economy; the discourse of economics from the early modern period onward and what it reveals about the culture of a particular period and place; and the economics of authorship itself, from early models of patronage to contemporary questions surrounding high art and mass consumption.

Economic Citizens to some extent takes all of these approaches. It pinpoints the ways Asians and Asian Americans have been represented through the lens of capitalist excess. It explicates the role of economic exchange in Asian American literature. It unravels Asian American criticism's ambivalent relationship to the consumption of Asian and Asian American culture. And finally it asks economic critics to consider how race complicates our reading of economics in literature.

The connection between linguistic representation and monetary representation lies at the heart of economic criticism, which has posited in different ways exactly how the two might be linked. Marc Shell identifies a number of different theories—that words and money each possess value; that words themselves function like credit-money or they work as commodities; that both words and coins transmit meaning. F. Ross-Landi, for example, applies Marx' theories of use and exchange value to language, arguing that the "message-content" of words stands as their use-value, a value that can only be calculated after exchange has occurred (see Osteen and Woodmansee, 14–15). Mark Osteen and Martha Woodmansee argue, however, that Ross-Landi's strict translation of use- and exchange-value serves primarily to demonstrate "that the structures of linguistic and economic systems are not identical, and so distinctions of definitions that hold for one 'economy' do not hold for another" (15). Critics like Shell, Osteen, and Woodmansee object to the uncritical pairing of words and money and to incautious attempts to substitute economic metaphors for linguistic ones. Instead they highlight research that focuses on structural similarities, shared histories and origins, or "homologies between language and money"(Osteen and Woodmansee, 15).

Jean-Joseph Goux is particularly notable for his claims of an "isomorphic" relationship between various systems (*Symbolic Economies*, 21).[13] Tracing carefully Marx's development of the money form, he recalls Marx's analysis of the four stages that take place. The first consists of the generalized form of exchange in which one object is made equivalent to the next. The second development is the move toward an "extended form of value," in which all objects are placed into relationship with all other objects. Such an arrangement is unsatisfactory, as both Goux and Marx explain, as the infinite number of relationships is not ordered in any manner. Goux writes, "[The commodity] is caught in the interminable contradictions of a *relativism* in which no one component prevails, which has no 'unitary phenomenon form'" (*Symbolic Economies,* 15). In the third stage, the chaos is resolved through the naming of a "general equivalent," which in the commodity world is gold. And in the fourth stage, the general equivalent is consolidated as "the manifold world of commodities becomes centered, centralized around what confers a value—a fixed worth, or price—on each commodity" (*Symbolic Economies,* 16). What makes Goux's work so ambitious, however, is his tracing of these four stages in systems involving not just products but signs, subjects, and objects. In a strategy that will not be persuasive to all readers, he carefully draws comparisons between the hierarchies that structure psychoanalysis, social systems, and religious systems, arguing that each and all evolve through the same four stages that Marx ascribes to the commodity world. They begin with the moment of identification, and progress from the creation of a chain of identification, to the naming of a general equivalent, and the consolidation around that equivalent.

Like economic critics who make visible the shared histories, structures, and logic between diverse systems such as economics, linguistics, and social organizations, I too argue for a link between economic circulation and the social circulation and definition of Asian Americans.[14] While I am not claiming that the two systems are analogous or that the terms of one might be substituted for the other, I do argue that the two systems share a logic and a language of loss, gain, compensation, excess, abstraction, reconciliation, equivalence, and equality. The literature that I examine depends on the system of economic exchange to articulate abstract citizenship and to construct an idealized relationship to the nation-state. Monetary exchange and the structures and social agreements that enable that exchange to take place offer an overt and acceptable means for Asian Americans to assert their membership within the imagined American community. Perhaps even more importantly, it also suggests a logic by which representation and social equivalence can be made manifest. What is seen as foreign, alien, unassimilable, and invisible is thus, seemingly, through the logic of universal equivalence, rendered the same, comprehensible and translatable. We see here the very moment in which "Asian Americanness" appears—a moment that is only possible because of its articulation in relation to something else.

Economic Citizens also calls into question how race might challenge traditional applications of economic criticism. The most common intersections between critical race theory and economic criticism revolve around slavery and the appropriation of black bodies as property. My work argues that not only have racialized peoples functioned as property or labor in the production of capital, but race itself exposes the contradictions and the intense effort behind effecting economic exchange and uniformity, thus undermining rather than supporting the logic of universal equivalence. And it also demonstrates that the economic realm is itself culturally and racially determined. Defined as alien to African Americans even as it comprises the sole terrain and occupation of Asian Americans, economic exchange does not operate in uniform ways for all peoples. In short, how does our understanding and reading of money as sign change when the agents of commodity exchange are racialized or when we realize that racialized peoples have themselves functioned as a symbol of money's circulation?

In the texts I examine we find two parallel narratives—an economic one alternately vacillating between an equitable and controlled circulation of goods and services and anxiety over stolen money, undervalued objects, and wasted labor power, while a more visible "racialized" narrative revolves around loss, social or familial alienation, cultural conflict, transformation, and resolution. By demonstrating the dependence of the more visible narrative of Asian American difference on the less noted but, I would argue, more central story of economic upheaval, *Economic Citizens* argues: 1) that economics play a significant role in mainstream constructions of Asians and Asian Americans while also structuring the logic of universal equivalence and wholeness within Asian American narratives themselves; and 2) that mainstream Asian American literature offers a compelling economic undercurrent that undermines the texts' presumed messages of racial healing as well as much larger assumptions regarding the predictability of economic exchange and the ability to move easily between the economic, social, and symbolic realms.

Asian American Literary Studies and the Logic of Economic Exchange

The logic of economics has also played a role in the reading of Asian American literature. In the last three decades the growth of Asian

American culture has been seen as a primary means of establishing American identity and presence. It has been an important counterhegemonic strategy and a founding premise of the field that the production of Asian American art politically empowers the larger Asian American community. Seen as a response to the silencing and erasure of Asian Americans' histories in the United States, the appearance of Asian American cultural production has largely been heralded as a sign of progressive change. Particularly in the 1990s, critics pointed to the positive attention that Asian American writers had received from publishers, newspaper editors, awards committees, and anthology editors. In her foreword to *Reading the Literatures of Asian America,* Elaine Kim notes:

> At the moment, we are experiencing the start of a golden age of Asian American cultural production. Beginning around 1983 and continuing into the present, Asian American writers of diverse ancestries have burst into the U.S. cultural scene with novels, poetry, plays, short stories, and book-length critical studies written from a wide array of perspectives that reflect the increasing heterogeneity of contemporary Asian American communities. (xi)

In the same volume, Shirley Geok-lin Lim and Amy Ling add, "Asian American writers have been extremely productive, often garnering national awards and international recognition" (3). Sau-ling Wong also begins her important book-length study, *Reading Asian American Literature*, by establishing the active work of Asian American writers and critics.

> A number of book-length studies by Asian American critics have appeared or are forthcoming, and recent publishing projects to broaden the canon of American literature have all, to varying extents, included Asian American authors. ... In the half decade preceding the writing of this study, there have appeared a large number of first novels, most of them well received; new novels by established writers;

> several award-winning short story collections; many other interesting additions to Asian American literature; anthologies of Asian American writing, especially by and/or about women; a Broadway hit; and many volumes of poetry, several of which garnered national honors. (3)

While Asian American critics like Kim, Lim, Ling, and Wong reference this Asian American "renaissance" as a means of signaling a new era in Asian American literary history and of questioning how Asian American critics might respond to these new developments, I would argue that the prodigious production has not waited for critics' interpretation but has instead lent itself easily and immediately to the writing of a new literary history, one determined by the prominence of Asians in the global economy. In their respective anthologies of Asian American literature, editors (and authors) Shawn Wong and Jessica Hagedorn each construct a narrative in which the past exclusion of Asian Americans has given way to a new global reality. In his introduction to *Asian American Literature*, one of a series of anthologies devoted to multicultural literature published by HarperCollins, Shawn Wong outlines repeatedly the history of discrimination and racism that Asian Americans face, and frames his anthology selections within that history. Situating Asian American literature in both a national and global context, Wong details the history of anti-Asian sentiment from the early exclusion acts to World War II and to the Korean War, detailing what he terms the trajectory from "yellow peril to red menace" (2). Wong notes that such a hostile climate toward Asian Americans allowed for only a narrow range of Asian American literature to reach mainstream audiences. Such a climate, he argues, has since undergone substantial shifts, and although anti-Asian violence persists, the United States' changing demographics as well as the new global economy demand that Americans be educated within a multicultural framework:

> The business community, advertising and marketing agencies, and all levels of education are in desperate need of resources, people, and books that can educate workers and

> management, teachers, and executives about our changing cultural identity. . . . American corporations have been competing on a global and multicultural level for years while much of America's educational curriculum remains monocultural." (4)

Wong's creation of an Asian American anthology thus addresses a variety of deficits: It challenges the lack of Asian American cultural representation, or the limitation of those representations to stereotypes, as well as Americans' needs for an education that addresses more adequately current economic realities. Wong's introductory narrative replicates a similar logic to that found in Asian American literature itself. It is permeated with the language of loss and surplus, deficiency and excess. His juxtaposition of Asian American cultural representation with the insistent demands of businesses rushing to adapt to the new global economy demonstrates that such cultural production is most clearly understood within the framework of production in general—the need for corporations to employ a diverse workforce, to attract a multicultural audience, to compete within a global marketplace. The creation of an Asian American anthology that relies on the logic of economic equivalence reiterates the link that Asian American writers themselves assert: The creation of an Asian and/or Asian American culture and identity depends on and in turn constitutes economic circulation and community.

Jessica Hagedorn's anthology *Charlie Chan Is Dead: An Anthology of Contemporary Asian American Fiction* depends on a different but related logic—that excess itself stands as a sign of social equality. Published in 1993, *Charlie Chan Is Dead* proclaims itself as "the first anthology of Asian American fiction by a commercial publisher in this country" (xxviii). Hagedorn, like Wong, introduces the anthology with a discussion of how Asian American culture has historically been perceived. Explaining the anthology's title, she writes, "Charlie Chan is as much a part of the demeaning legacy of stereotypes that includes Fu Manchu, Stepin' Fetchit, Sambo, Aunt Jemima, Amos N' Andy, Speedy Gonzalez, Tonto, and Little Brown Brother" (xxi–xxii). The list of stereotypes is only one of a number of inventories that Hagedorn makes (others include itemizations of "canonical" literatures—works by writers of color, Asian American writers, and finally the forty-eight writers included in *Charlie Chan Is Dead*) and the themes of abundance, excess, and diversity define the essay. Hagedorn makes it clear that the anthology itself is not bound by a narrow set of criteria.

> The writers selected for this anthology are exhilarating in their differences; there is an array of cultural backgrounds, age range, and literary styles gathered here. No "theme" was imposed on the writers when they were invited to submit. I let it be known that I was definitely more interested in "riskier" work, and that I was eager to subvert the very definition of what was considered "fiction." (xxviii)

She continues to emphasize the diversity of the selections, and the anthology's resistance to singularity by citing the authors' varied geographic and ethnic backgrounds. "Some were born in the Philippines, some in Seattle. A few in Hawaii. Others in Toronto or London. Some live in San Francisco. Oakland. Stockton. Los Angeles. New York City. Santa Fe. Family in Panama. Singapore. Tokyo. Manila. Pusan. Chicago. Hayward. Boston. Brooklyn. Beijing. Mindoro. Washington, D.C. Seoul. Greeley, Colorado. India. Penang. Moscow, Idaho." She concludes by arguing, "Asian American literature? Too confining a term, maybe. World literature? Absolutely" (xxix–xxx). Sau-ling Wong has pointed to Hagedorn's embrace of transnationalism, and has questioned the efficacy of loosening Asian American literature from its national moorings.[15] While I agree with Wong's questioning of a transnational framework for situating Asian American Studies, what is equally of interest to me here is Hagedorn's dependence on the profusion of Asian American literature and authors, an extravagance that works to counteract the proliferation of narrow stereotyping. While Shawn Wong suggests that knowledge of Asian American culture is necessary to compete effectively in today's global economy, Hagedorn instead uses the language of global excess to remap Asian America. Her naming of the numerous and diverse places of Asian American authorial origin, even as it disrupts any assumptions that "Asian America" can be reduced to a handful of ethnic identities, essentially replicates the language of global transit, and suggests that Asian Americans—like other peoples, commodities, and information—are moving easily across cultural and geographic borders. Hagedorn's claim to the title of "world literature," I would argue, not only slips the national boundaries that have traditionally defined Asian American literature, but it also implicitly grounds this literature within the general logic of global capitalism. The proliferation of Asian American literatures—in terms of genre and/or ethnic or regional diversity—becomes simply another realm in which the rapid production of global commodities signals the arrival of a new economic era.

If Asian Americans had previously been erased from what had traditionally constituted "American" history or culture, the rise of Asian economies, the larger numbers of Asian immigrants to the United States, and the increasing visibility of Asians in U.S. political and cultural institutions has enabled a narrative of Asian American literary production and consumption that moves from lack to surplus, or to use Sau-ling Wong's paradigm, from "necessity" to "extravagance." Although certainly it is true that Asian American writing is being published and read more now than ever, I am questioning how this narrative from "less" to "more" coincides with other forms of referencing Asian economic surplus, whether in terms of class or the late twentieth-century vivid imaginings of the large number of Asian workers, Asian immigrants, Asian monies, and Asian commodities. And finally, I suggest that surplus becomes a common means of establishing Asian American subjectivity, one that only underscores and enables the language of American equivalence.

If Asian American critics have read the production of Asian American literature as a largely positive move, the consumption of Asian American works has been greeted with far more skepticism.[16] Asian American critics have mainly shared bell hooks' concerns that consumption occurs only through the erasure of difference. In her careful and illuminating essay on the phenomenal success of Amy Tan's books, Sau-ling Wong writes of Tan's second novel, *The*

Kitchen God's Wife, that the ethnographic comparisons between "the" Chinese and U.S. cultures that the main (Chinese) character offers her daughter are "not empirically grounded contrast, but the kind of cultural tidbits Orientalist readers enjoy—decontextualized, overgeneralized, speculative, and confirmative of essential difference" ("Sugar Sisterhood,"198). Essentialism and decontextualization reappear in Sunaina Maira's comments about the current consumption of what she calls "Indo-chic." She writes, "Ethnic difference, specifically coded as the essence of South Asian 'culture,' can be consumed and made safe, in a sense, its threatening foreignness now neutralized."[17] Perhaps most well-known, however, are the arguments made by Frank Chin, Jeffery Chan, Lawson Inada, and Shawn Wong in the preface to the first anthology of Asian American literature, *Aiiieeeee!!!: An Anthology of Asian-American Writers.* The editors frame their selections against the specter of mass consumption and explicitly note that the works included in *Aiiieeeee!!!* have not enjoyed the kind of mainstream success that other Asian American writers (mainly Chinese American) have found. They denounce writers like Pardee Lowe, Jade Snow Wong, C. Y. Lee, Virginia Lee (the writers on which I focus in the first chapter), and Maxine Hong Kingston for their widespread popularity, accusing them of fulfilling white readers' fantasies of an exotic Orient and of portraying Asians as foreign, alien, and unassimilable. In their preface, they argue that writers like Lin Yutang and C. Y. Lee "consciously set out to become American, in the white sense of the word, and succeeded in becoming 'Chinese American' in the stereotypical sense of the good, loyal, obedient, passive, law-abiding, cultured sense of the word. It is no surprise that their writing is from whiteness, not from Chinese America. Becoming white supremacist was part of their consciously and voluntarily becoming 'American'" (x). In their introduction to Chinese and Japanese American literature, they explain that writers like John Okada were ignored by the publishing industry and mainstream audiences because "authentic" Asian American literature relied on unfamiliar tropes, structures, and languages to describe Asians' experiences in the United States. In a jibe against C. Y. Lee's *The Flower Drum Song,* which was adapted into a Rodgers and Hammerstein musical, the editors write of John Okada's *No-No Boy* that "Depression, despairing, death, suicide, listless anger, and a general tone of low-key hysteria closed inside the gray of a constant overcast and drizzling Seattle pervade the book. Definitely not the stuff of a musical" (Aiiieeeee!!!, xxxix).

Asian American literary criticism has been divided on exactly how Asian American literature operates within mainstream and dominant ideologies and institutions, and on the level of resistance it might offer. In her discussion of Asian American literature and its relationship to the larger U.S. canon, Lisa Lowe argues that an Asian American aesthetic by its very definition resists resolution and assimilation. Despite differences in form, content, and voice, Lowe reads Asian American literature as a whole as an aesthetic "defined by contradiction, not sublimation, such that discontent, nonequivalence, and irresolution call into question the project of abstracting the aesthetic as a separate domain of unification and reconciliation" (44). Working against critics who question the consumption of literature by writers of color, and who suggest that such consumption results in the erasure or essentializing of otherness, Lowe, as I read her, argues instead that literature by writers of color inherently defies such incorporation.

If Lowe argues that Asian American literature is defined by "nonequivalence"—an argument that my own readings support—other Asian American literary critics have argued that we have not yet recognized fully our complicity in reading and valuing Asian American literature though the logic of capital. In other words, while Lowe's work offers us a means of understanding Asian American literature in fundamental opposition to exchange, critics such as Viet Nguyen and Tomo Hattori suggest instead that we need to be more cognizant of how our criticism cannot escape cooptation, institutionalization, and the imperative of capitalist exchange. Nguyen writes, "For the Asian American intellectual class, it is racial identity as a mode of resistance to capitalist exploitation that accrues symbolic rather than economic capital" (5). Hattori argues similarly that "The jouis-sense of Asian American resistance, the moment in which it materializes its resisting subject, is the moment in which

Asian American criticism enjoys its own trauma, produces it as excess and surplus, and coins it as ethnic cultural capital" (232). Hattori characterizes his own project this way: "My method of reading, then, looks 'for the money' and 'for the bottom line' in Asian American literature and criticism to expose, confirm, and value the discourse of being Asian in America that emerges from the Asian American subject's undeluded and pragmatic manipulation of herself as a human form of racial capital" (231). For Hattori, Asian American critics have failed to realize that idealized notions of a resistant minority only support the hegemonic structures already in place and ignore the ways that global capitalism has inexorably and powerfully defined the Asian American subject. I am sympathetic to Hattori's arguments, and I too look for "the money." My project, however, focuses not so much on the need to recognize our own cooptation by capital, but to look more closely at how Asian American writers depend on and yet disrupt the logic of economic exchange as a means of constructing and rewriting their own racialized identities. Here I echo critic Miranda Joseph, when she remarks, "As I see it, the issue here is not so much the commodification of discourse, of media, art, and information, but the discursivity of the commodity" (34).

It seems to me then that the question of whether Asian American culture operates according to principles of nonequivalence or equivalence can only be answered in the affirmative; that by reading Asian American culture through the logic of economic exchange, we can see that nonequivalence *and* equivalence are always happening simultaneously. Asian Americanization is a tale of abstraction, exchange, universalization, circulation, and embodiment, but it is also a narrative of alienation, difference, and disenfranchisement. As Karen Shimakawa writes, "For what characterizes Asian Americanness as it comes into visibility . . . is its constantly shifting relation to Americanness, a movement between visibility and invisibility, foreignness and domestication/assimilation; it is that *movement between* enacted by and on Asian Americans, I argue, that marks the boundaries of Asian American cultural (and sometimes legal) citizenship" (3). The logic of economic exchange not only makes that movement particularly *visible,* but we can see in the works of Asian American writers and in the consumption of those works by mainstream readers that it is the logic that makes that movement *possible.*

Economic Citizens thus constructs the history of that relationship, tracing the characterization of Asians as symbolic of excessive or inappropriate exchange and unveiling the deployment of economic exchange within Asian American literature itself as an ultimately futile means of constructing identity and writing Asians into the larger American community. It also offers a way of reading and contextualizing the consumption of Asian American culture in a manner that acknowledges the economic and discursive structures that make "Asian American" comprehensible, and suggests that readings of Asian American literature can recognize its tendencies toward equivalence even as the specter of nonequivalence constantly looms. The book moves largely chronologically, structured by the most visible economic threats that Asians have posed to to the nation over the last fifty years. As such, the project primarily focuses on Chinese and Japanese American texts. I have chosen to use the term *Asian American* in my title, however, not to erase unconsciously the differences and histories that are contained and contested within Asian America, but because "Asia" as a whole has been imagined to represent the threat of cheap labor, excessive consumption, and global capitalism run amuck. What is being negotiated in terms of identity is not an articulation of ethnicity but one of race and even more specifically of difference in general. For when Jing-mei Woo pronounces at the end of Amy Tan's *The Joy Luck Club*, "And now I see what part of me is Chinese" (331), we understand that what she has recognized is not anything that references a specific Chinese ethnicity or history, politics, or culture, but instead calls forth a more comprehensive and essential difference and "humanity."

In a time during which Chineseness signaled the specter of communism, popular Chinese American texts of the 1950s and 1960s—Jade Snow Wong's *Fifth Chinese Daughter*, C. Y. Lee's *The Flower Drum Song*, Pardee Lowe's *Father and Glorious Descendant*, and Virginia Lee's *The House that Tai Ming Built*—all assertively position Chinese labor and products as vital elements of a vigorous and growing ethnic and national economy. These texts are the focus of my first chapter, in which I investigate how Chineseness has been marketed and produced. I focus particularly on the circulation of cultural commodities as a means of defining Chinatown's geographic boundaries, thereby marking the economic and cultural position of Chinese Americans within the United States. Crowded with objects, food, furniture, merchants, and servants, Chinatown stands as a symbol of gentility and old world traditions, even as each narrative is filled with and dominated by efforts to produce, exchange, and consume products, labor, and capital. The mainstream reader's consumption of Chinese American difference and exotica thus in fact marks a process by which Chinese Americans articulate their Americanness through the establishment of an alternative marketplace in which Asian American identity can be assessed, valued, and made commensurate with other U.S. commodities.

The "tsunami" of Japanese capitalism in the late eighties forms the backdrop for the works I examine in Chapter 2, in which I read the travel narratives of Japanese American writers who "return" to Japan. Looking at works by David Mura and Lydia Minatoya, I trace the embodiment of value within everyday objects, and assess the economic exchange effected in their journeys across Japan and other Asian countries, exchange that ultimately enables healing and homecoming. Blurring the boundaries between the local and the global, countries such as Japan, China, and Nepal, as well as art itself, are transformed into sites of resistance as well as universalization against which the past conflicts between the United States and Asia and Asian America (e.g., the Vietnam War, the internment of Japanese Americans) can be resolved. The cultural versatility that is gained when Minatoya and Mura cross historical, geographical, and national boundaries becomes a sign of simultaneous global universality and national acceptance, and a confirmation of the United States as a symbol for a multicultural and international community.

In Chapter 3, I look more carefully at how the language of capital overdetermines the creation of specifically female Asian American subjectivities. Examining the rhetoric of exchange that dominates discussions about Asian mail-order brides, I argue that mainstream media representations of the growing practice of mail-order marriages repeatedly voice anxiety about the presence of money—the brokers' fees, the groom's payments, the bride's poverty—while the international matchmaking organizations themselves use the logic of global capital to naturalize the immigration of Asian women into the U.S. home. I contrast these representations with that of Wanwadee Larsen's memoir, *Confessions of a Mail-Order Bride*. Larsen romantically underscores Asian "values" as a means of escaping the concrete economic valuing of her labor as wife; nevertheless, she cannot avoid entirely the logic and language of exchange as a means of defining the Thai American woman's identity.

In the final chapter, I move from U.S. citizenship to global citizenship and explore how multinational belonging is rendered possible through a locating of value within Chinese women's bodies and histories. Contextualizing the works within the twenty-first century threat of China's exponential economic expansion, and examining such works as Adeline Yen Mah's bestselling *Falling Leaves: The Memoir of an Unwanted Chinese Daughter*, Pang-Mei Natasha Chang's *Bound Feet & Western Dress*, and May-lee Chai and Winberg Chai's *The Girl from Purple Mountain*, I interrogate the current fascination with works that posit the resilience of Chinese women against the traumatic events of twentieth century Chinese history. These memoirs—all written in English, published by mainstream U.S. presses, and sold in U.S. markets—almost all uniformly tell the story of the path of capital gone astray. Thus, although the works in unison make mention of historical events such as the Boxer Rebellion, the creation of the Republic, the Japanese invasion of China, the rise of the Communist Party and of cultural practices (that highlight a repressive Chinese patriarchy), such as the binding of feet and the taking of concubines, the plots themselves revolve around the circulation, loss, and recovery of monies and objects. The figure of the (suffering) Chinese woman expatriate thus offers us a means of demonstrating the links between female and feminist subjectivity, twentieth century Chinese history, global citizenship, and the circuits of (global) capital.

In the texts of *Economic Citizens* we can see the strict boundaries that separate exotic Chinatown from mainstream America, that define the tragic (but triumphant) masses of China against a U.S. modernity, that delineate Japanese worldliness in the face of American provincialism, that position "third-world" need against first-world generosity. And yet, all of these works are obsessed with circulation; and the movement of objects, people, and money gestures toward their own attempts at social border crossings even when actual transfer might be impossible. The narratives' progress and tensions often also depend on the circulation of women, an emphasis that reveals the gendered dynamics underlying the creation of Asian American subjectivities through capital. Women's efforts to keep monies and objects moving, along with their own navigation within patriarchal systems of exchange, make visible the necessity of preserving the ideals of family and nation as a means of ensuring the development of capital. They in fact can often ensure that such circulation remains mappable and controllable, a means of delineating the boundaries of "home," even one that spans continents. As the project of tracking the circulation of capital, commodities, and people has become increasingly difficult, as capital itself has become more flexible and adept at manipulating global, local, and national interests for its own benefit, mapping the circulation of and within Asian American texts enables a clearer sense of how movement itself can be effected between the realms of race, nation, and "world."

1 The Promise of Exchange

Production, Circulation, and Consumption within Chinatown Ethnographies

Early in his 1943 memoir, *Father and Glorious Descendant*, Pardee Lowe declares of his father's thriving Chinatown business, "A new economic activity was born" (8). Although Lowe refers here to the creation of his father's dry-goods store, which becomes a focal point for Chinatown commerce, he might well have also been speaking of the birth of a new Asian American literary economy as well. A national bestseller, this narrative of a successful San Francisco merchant was just one of a number of highly popular Chinese American books that detailed Chinatown life.[1] Offering an alternative perspective to their U.S. audiences, demoralized from the 1949 victory of Mao and the declaration of a communist China, these works are often procapitalist and revolve around the workings of Chinatown businesses. They document the lives of Chinatown residents, relying primarily on lengthy descriptions of "strange" Chinese food, elaborate ceremonies and holiday celebrations, filial piety, and "Confucian" morals and values. Largely ethnographic in approach, they also assiduously carve out the social space of Chinatown, marking its geographic and cultural borders for large U.S. audiences, and in effect creating an identifiable Chinatown culture.

Operating alongside the economics of publishing Chinatown memoirs are the extensive economies within the texts themselves.

The drama of money—its earning, movement, accumulation, and loss—permeates every page. While these works have largely been dismissed by contemporary Asian American critics as pandering to and confirming assumptions about unassimilable Chinese difference or Chinese capitalist desires, this chapter maps the production, circulation, and consumption of Chinatown labor, monies, and goods within these texts and argues that the narratives of exchange that structure these works both articulate a Chinese American identity and enable the commensurability of that difference, an equation that promises even as it complicates the possibility of Asian American citizenship.

Later dubbed "Chinatown Tour Guides" by critic Sau-ling C. Wong, memoirs such as Pardee Lowe's *Father and Glorious Descendant* (1943) and Jade Snow Wong's *Fifth Chinese Daughter* (1943; reprinted 1950) as well as novels such as C. Y. Lee's *The Flower Drum Song* (1957) and Virginia Lee's *The House That Tai Ming Built* (1960)[2] have all been criticized for their essentialist and Orientalist portraits of Chinese Americans—they have been held up not as paradigms of early Asian American literature but instead as propaganda that has contributed to the marginalization of Asian Americans. As I mention in the previous chapter, editors Frank Chin, Jeffery Chan, Lawson Inada, and Shawn Wong hold a particularly dim view of these writers.

> World War II signaled the suppression of a Japanese-American writing movement that had been active since the late twenties and the sudden popularity of Chinese-Americans' writing to encourage America to "assimilate her loyal minorities," as the dust jacket of Pardee Lowe's *Father and Glorious Descendant* states. The implied worth of these first Chinese-Americans to reach mass print and enjoy a degree of popularity was that they mostly had patriotic virtues rather than literary ones. They were more manipulable. (xxii)

Aiiieeeee! is itself a forceful response to the popularity of these early Asian American writers, an attempt to provide a voice that problematized rather than eased the relationship of Asian America to the U.S. nation-state. Critic David Leiwei Li is more understanding of the reasons behind such exotic depictions of Chinatown and works to situate these texts against the social and historical pressures the authors faced: "The assimilationist effort was largely a trapped and cornered reaction—the life of Chinese Americans without political rights is subhuman and a living death—and the wish to affirm Chinese humanity by resorting to an unpracticed ancestral high culture is an understandable but still pathetic gesture" (322).

In her discussion of Pardee Lowe's and Jade Snow Wong's memoirs, Sau-ling Wong identifies the genre's rhetorical devices. She points to the authors' steady use of the pronoun "you" when addressing readers, and to some of the chapter titles in which readers are directed to presumable customs and practices of Chinese peoples in the United States. Drawing on the already fixed assumptions of their white readers about the "ahistorical, almost genetic, Chinese essence to all persons of Chinese ancestry regardless of their upbringing," these writers then speak from the "native's" point of view. She adds, "Although there is much else in Lowe's and Wong's books besides these gestures of consideration for the sensibilities of white readers, it is undeniable that both of these authors, like their Chinese-born counterparts, are conscious of their role as cultural interpreters who can obtain a measure of recognition from whites for the insider's insight they can offer" ("Autobiography as Guided Chinatown Tour?," 40–41).

Each of these descriptions pinpoints and critiques the use of a static notion of Chinese culture as a means of achieving recognition and acceptance from their white audiences. While I agree that much of these writers' approaches depends on the commodification of an "ancient" and exotic Chinese culture, the narratives' anxiety of how commodities in general are produced, circulated, and consumed belies their seemingly confident strategy. The circulation of workers, products, and money becomes representative of larger questions about Chinese Americans' social circulation, within and outside the borders of Chinatown. Underlying their ethnographic descriptions of Chinese customs and traditions are other narratives of exchange, transactions that ask us to consider not just what is being disseminated—exotic stereotypes—but instead how dissemination operates. As Chinese Americans imagine themselves for the first time as American citizens, they demonstrate that the establishment of exchange becomes a prerequisite to claiming national identity.

I focus on the four aforementioned texts, Pardee Lowe's *Father and Glorious Descendant* (1943), Jade Snow Wong's *Fifth Chinese Daughter* (1950), C. Y. Lee's *The Flower Drum Song* (1957), and Virginia Lee's *The House That Tai Ming Built* (1960). These works span the era between the repeal of exclusion and the Immigration Act of 1965 and were recognized by audiences outside of Chinatown. Published by nationally known publishing houses, all were also reviewed in national newspapers such as the *New York Times*. Whereas both *Father and Glorious Descendant* and *The Flower Drum Song* were bestsellers, *The Flower Drum Song* also became a 1959 Rodgers and Hammerstein musical and a Hollywood film in 1961 and has most recently been adapted into a Broadway play by David Henry Hwang. Jade Snow Wong's *Fifth Chinese Daughter* continues to be included in high school and college curricula and perhaps has received the most attention from Asian American literary critics. The books all follow a similar format: Located in San Francisco's Chinatown, they revolve around intercultural and often intergenerational conflict. Usually a struggle between the family's patriarch and the more "Americanized" daughter or son, the tensions ostensibly center on the elder generation's inability to forsake their "queer" Chinese habits. The books thus attempt to negotiate the borders surrounding Chinatown, defining them, interpreting its customs for the audiences that lie outside of those boundaries, and simulating both easy and arduous movement across its geographical limits. Equally important, the works deploy similar economic narratives; we see in each book a trajectory toward more widespread economic exchange, by which each narrator enables his or her own abstraction toward citizenship. The objects that they produce, the monies that they circulate, the commodities that are purchased by others all become a means for their own claiming of an American identity, their own circulation within a larger national sphere, and their own consumption into the national body politic. I begin with Jade Snow Wong's transfer of labor power from within the family to a larger national marketplace; I then move to a discussion of how the circulation of Chinatown goods, services, and monies are effected or limited within the works of Pardee Lowe and C. Y. Lee; and I conclude with an analysis of Virginia Lee's *The House that Tai Ming Built* and its troubling conclusions about consumption as a means of integration.

She Works Hard for Her Money: Making Chinese Women's Labor Visible

First published in 1950, Jade Snow Wong's memoir *Fifth Chinese Daughter* focuses on the experiences of the fifth daughter of a Chinese American factory owner. Documenting Wong's life in the early 1930s of San Francisco's Chinatown, the memoir begins by outlining the borders of Chinatown's geography. Situating her readers in Nob Hill, Wong alerts us that from there, "tourists and curio-seekers in a bare three minutes can stroll from the city's fashionable shopping district into the heart of Old China" (1). Wong creates a boundary between Chinatown and the rest of San Francisco, and suggests to the reader that a narrative and landscape shift is taking place here, in which she will be transported to another place and time.

While the memoir ostensibly serves as a means of tracing Jade Snow's life from childhood into early adulthood and of enlightening "Western" readers on the cultural values and traditions of Chinese/Chinese Americans (Wong seldom makes the distinction), the memoir also can be mapped through the labor that Jade Snow performs. Divided into five stages—the labor for her family, for other (white) families, for a college, for the nation, and finally for herself as a writer and potter—the work enables Jade Snow's assertion of self and community. While her domestic labor for her own and other families results in her silencing, the other forms of work enable her to find "voice," one heard only outside the confines of her family and Chinatown. The linking of "voice" to labor, that voice can only be achieved through non-Chinatown labor, demonstrates the interconnections between identity, economic exchange, and ethnography. Any efforts to move outside of Chinatown into the larger national public sphere depend not only on one's role as expert on and translator of all things Chinese but also on one's ability as a worker to adapt and to produce in a variety of conditions. The surplus value that Wong produces for her employers does not, however, take the form of economic capital but cultural capital; in each job she gains further knowledge of the differences between the United States and Chinatown—indeed the actual work she is supposed to do seems secondary to her production of knowledge—and it is through that knowledge (and more importantly through that labor) that Chinese Americanness is produced.

The spectacle of Jade Snow's labor as well as that of her family is asserted from the start of the memoir. Because her family lives in the back of their garment factory, work and home life are very much intertwined. Even as Wong describes the process by which the clothes are made, she also uses this overlap as a means of explaining to her readers the position of women in Chinese society.

> While most Chinese women in San Francisco still had to conform to the Old-World custom of staying at home, her father believed that according to New World Christian ideals women had a right to work to improve the economic status of their family. Because they couldn't come to the factory, Mr. Wong took their work to them, installed and maintained their sewing machines, taught them how to sew, and collected the finished overalls. (5)

Wong thus redefines the augmentation of the family's labor power as her father's battle for women's empowerment, while simultaneously opposing the static and outdated ("Old-World") assumptions of Chinese peoples with the more progressive and "Christian" beliefs of her father. She also frames work as a "right," an entitlement granted by "New World Christian ideals." Despite her father's "modern" views, however, Wong represents her parents as the source of the exploitation of her labor. Their "rigid" Chinese guidelines for child-rearing, studying, working, and even for such mundane tasks as cooking and shopping, serve as the backdrop from which she can assert her American independence, the right to work for others and eventual achievement of self-employment: "At eleven, this daughter could hardly find a moment of her life which was not accounted for, and accounted for properly, by Mama or Daddy" (65). The meticulous calculations of time and the disciplining of Jade Snow parallel the other precise formulas and routines that the Wong family employs for every event, from weddings to funerals, and from the cooking of rice to the celebrating of Chinese New Year.

Wong's resistance to her parents' dominance is predicated on a number of factors. Leslie Bow points to its reliance on the rhetoric of women's empowerment. She notes, "Highlighting the convergence between American individualism and the advocation of women's autonomy, equal rights, and access to education allows Jade Snow to constitute her 'unfilial piety'—the break she makes with her Chinese family—as gendered (if not exactly feminist) resistance" (*Betrayal and Other Acts of Subversion*, 79). Wong's embracing of "American individualism" is particularly grounded in her emphasis on work, and she effects her gendered resistance through our assumptions about different kinds of labor and how it should be compensated. Wong particularly distinguishes between unrecognized domestic labor in the family and her much more visible work for other families, Mills university, the United States government, and eventually herself. Her early descriptions of work within the home focus on its tedious and overwhelming nature.

> She did the family washing in big galvanized buckets in the bathtub. Bed linens and Daddy's shirts were sent out, as well as Big Brother's laundry but Jade Snow washed all the underwear, night clothes, sweaters, blouses, dresses, and towels for herself, Younger Sister, Daddy, Mama, and Forgiveness. She also dusted the rooms and swept them thoroughly, and about once a month did extras like cleaning the woodwork, polishing the aluminum kettles, and giving the big stove a good scouring. . . . For the chores which Jade Snow did, Mama paid her fifty cents a week. (70)

The exhaustive list ostensibly provides an "insider's" glimpse into the daily lives of a Chinese family, but equally importantly, Wong's excruciatingly detailed narration seeks to emphasize the endless nature of gendered labor. Unlike future economic exchanges in the memoir, the work Jade Snow does for her family is compensated only with money while her description highlights its routine and indistinguishable nature.

Jade Snow ultimately uses labor and the rise in value of labor power as a means of breaking free from her parents' discipline and establishing her own identity. She tells them, "You expect me to work my way through college—which would not have been possible in China. You expect me to exercise judgment in choosing my employers and my jobs and in spending my own money in the American world. Then why can't I choose my friends. . . . You must give me the freedom to find some answers for myself" (129). Jade Snow's claiming of her own labor power—her ability to earn and spend her own money—enables her to assert her independence. Like the younger generations in *The Flower Drum Song* and *The House That Tai Ming Built*, Jade Snow uses capitalism to move outside of the social borders of Chinatown—even as capitalism serves to restrict the older generation to those boundaries—and to offer new definitions of Chinese Americanness.

Jade Snow's labor enables her not only to break away from her identity within the family, but also to adopt the role of ethnographer and translator. Her first jobs for "American" families enable her to delineate the differences between their and her family life. She begins, however, with another lengthy description of the many tasks that make up her week.

> Jade Snow's new duties included keeping all the house clean (heavy and light cleaning), all the laundry, with a spotless white shirt every day for Mr. Kaiser, and a fresh, starched cotton dress daily for each of the two girls, the care of linens, all the subsequent ironing, cooking the family breakfasts, helping to prepare dinner under Mrs. Kaiser's supervision, serving, washing all the dishes, caring for the dog, and telling

> stories to the children who trailed her as she worked, for six and a half days a week. . . . [S]he was often reminded by her employer that not many "school jobs" at that time offered twenty dollars per month in addition to room and board. (113)

Not only does this job pay significantly more than her work for her family—although Wong hints that it is still not adequate compensation—but Wong also adds

> Tedious and unending and tiring as the work was, Jade Snow gained more than just room and board and twenty dollars per month. For a considerable period of time, she was an intimate member of an American household, where she observed its occupants early and late, moving in a pattern completely different from her own Chinese background. (113)

These passages represent the narrative's pervasive tension regarding how her labor is to be valued, and the indeterminacy of labor's value in general. As she again painstakingly details her many duties as laundress, maid, nanny, and cook, Wong juxtaposes her many roles with her employer's emphasis on the advantages of her position. This continuous validation of her compensation only highlights the absence of Wong's own ability to declare her own worth, as well as the contradictions of how to value labor in general.

And yet Wong makes the argument that Jade Snow "gains more" for her labor power than money; she is also compensated by her increased knowledge of "American household" practices. Knowledge here becomes another means of payment, one not immediately elaborated in monetary terms, but ultimately, as we see when *Fifth Chinese Daughter* is published, possessing value nonetheless. We see here that labor become a crucial way for marking Jade Snow's trajectory toward "independence" and identity formation. She becomes an "intimate member of an American household" a title that cannot be used to refer to her membership within a Chinese household and one that loses meaning altogether without the ethnic qualifications. Wong's suggestion that her household labor is paid for by the identity she gains also functions as a means of asserting the material value of ethnic or racial knowledge, specifically as a means of payment or wage. The cultural capital that such knowledge brings, especially about Chinese peoples, becomes what Jade Snow primarily seeks to accumulate. Her relocation from her family and Chinatown and into the larger community and nation is thus predicated on finding labor that enables her to keep and to sell again the surplus value of racial knowledge that she creates.

The collapse between her ethnic identity and the work that she does becomes particularly evident in her position at Mills College. As part of her scholarship to college, she works in the dean's home. Not "merely a servant," as she puts it, Jade Snow discovers that the Mills students "were perpetually curious about her Chinese background and Chinese ideologies, and for the first time she began to formulate in her mind the constructive and delightful aspects of the Chinese culture to present to non-Chinese" (161). Particularly emblematic of Wong's use of labor as a means of establishing identity is her work as cook for a special party for a string quartet. In an unusual show of interest, her family becomes involved in the project as well, sending over cooking supplies while her sister becomes her assistant. And at the party itself, Wong writes, "For the first time Jade Snow felt an important participant in the role of hostess. . . . There was no talk about music, only about Chinese food. And Jade Snow ceased thinking of famous people as 'those' in a world apart. She had a glimpse of the truth, that the great people of any race are unpretentious, genuinely honest, and nonpatronizing in their interest in other human beings" (172–173). Wong's universalizing rhetoric, and the elevation of Jade Snow into "participant," comes specifically not out of the labor that she performs as "cook," but out of her work as a Chinese cook of Chinese food. Her labor becomes valuable only when it is marked as "Chinese," and her transformation into "individual" is predicated on her ability both to alienate herself from that labor and to construct the Chinese as alien.

Wong's making labor visible through race becomes problematic when she ignores the exploitation of racialized labor. She fails to see that race functions within capitalism to render workers invisible, especially in her descriptions of Mills College's "democratic" attitude.

> After all that she had heard about Mills being a rich girls' school, Jade Snow could not find who the rich girls were, for the student body dressed simply in sweaters, blouses, skirts, or wash dresses. Mills living was democratic living in the truest sense.... [Mills Hall] housed over a hundred girls, and its kitchen staff was entirely Chinese, some of them descendants of the first Chinese kitchen help who worked for the founders of the college. (157)

Although Jade Snow triumphantly declares that she is unable to identify the students by class, it seems clear that the students can be easily differentiated from the kitchen staff, who are "entirely Chinese" (Bow, *Betrayal and Other Acts of Subversion*, 81). Both Elaine Kim and Leslie Bow have pointed to this passage as standing in contradiction to Wong's argument about the reality of racial equality at Mills and in the nation as a whole. What I find striking about this passage, however, is also its emphasis on Chinese contributions to university history. We see here the fundamental premise of Wong's argument: Even as racial difference has marked and differentiated and contributed to the exploitation of Chinese American women's labor power, she uses their labor as a means of highlighting and rendering of value Chinese American experiences. Through their work, the staff becomes a part of Mills history.

Jade Snow's final jobs as potter and writer make fully visible her labor and translate that work into an expression of racial identity. The spectacle of the working racialized body is magnified when Jade Snow decides to create her pottery in the window of a Chinatown shop. Unlike her largely unrecognized domestic drudgery, this enterprise brings large, astonished audiences.

> From the first time she first threw down a ball of clay on the wheel, the street was packed. There were even people on the balconies across the street, and clinging to the telephone

> pole. Passing automobiles on narrow Grant Avenue stopped and held up traffic while the drivers watched. The first day, policemen came because they thought there might be a riot. Jade Snow could have an audience any time of the day or night on that busy street. (244)

This closing image of her hypervisiblity is a striking one. Focusing not on the products she creates, Wong instead closes her memoir with the celebrity she finds. Far from being an anonymous "fifth Chinese daughter," Wong achieves an über individualization, differentiating herself fully from all those who come to stare. The completion of her identity formation is predicated certainly on making as visible as possible her ethnic and racial difference as well as on her gendered resistance. It also depends wholly, however, on the transformation of Jade Snow's labor. Others' exploitation of her domestic work becomes transformed into her own exploitation of her Chineseness, an exchange that is not only more financially rewarding but also enables a social and cultural circulation through the publication of her memoir (although I concede that she ultimately, however, remains trapped in a window). Wong effectively achieves the full collapse of labor with ethnic identity production; she has transformed herself into both producer and commodity, and economic exchange enables her movement into the larger national community even as it fully commodifies her.

Circulating Chineseness: Moving Beyond Chinatown?

The movement of Jade Snow's labor from within the family into the realm of the larger public sphere parallels the outwardly expanding circles of exchange that define Pardee Lowe's *Father and Glorious Descendant*. This narrative seems particularly open to the criticism leveled against it by Asian American authors and critics. Made up of thirty-three chapters, each consists of one vignette describing Father's exploits in Chinatown and beyond and begins its title with

"Father," as in "Father Dons His Pigtail and Takes a Bride," "Father Takes a Bath," and "Father's Robes of Immortality." Documented carefully by his son Glorious Descendant, a.k.a. Pardee Lowe, Father's life serves as a model for Chinatown culture, rituals, and values, and the descriptions of family and community often employ a formal rhetoric that serves to situate Chinese American culture in the distant and ancient "East."

> At dawn, throughout the day, and before going to bed, we respectfully hailed our male elders with their proper titles. *Ah Bahk* (Senior Uncle), we called the graybeards, while the younger men were greeted as *Ah Sook,* Junior Uncle. When their womenfolk came visiting, we poured tea. We were duly silent in their presence. . . . At home our lives were a round of polite Oriental salutations and formal bowings and scrapings. (67)

At the same time, Lowe also documents his father's insistence that the family make full claim to their American citizenship. He names his children after political figures such as George C. Pardee, Alice Roosevelt, Helen Taft, Woodrow Wilson, and Thomas Riley Marshall; and Lowe points out that, "When questioned, [my father] would be most belligerent about his citizenship, asserting testily, 'I am an American!'" (4). While Lowe's memoir thus seems to move primarily between ethnographic accounts of Chinese culture and fervent declarations of allegiance to the United States, a curious subplot emerges. The primary tensions in the memoir are neither found in the ambivalence over national belonging, nor in the conflict between father and son (although these exist), but instead in the anxiety around the gain, preservation, and loss of money.

The logic of capital itself is the means by which Lowe establishes the Chinatown community itself and the larger global community to which its residents belong. He begins his narrative with a description of Father's origins in Sahn Kay Gawk in China. Lowe writes, "The chief asset of Sahn Kay Gawk, or The-Corner-of-the-Mountain-Where-the-Water-Falls, I was to discover, was her sturdy and nimble-witted manpower who poured overseas into Honolulu, Havana, Pago Pago, Panama, Singapore, Sydney, Batavia, and San Francisco" (3). While readers are captivated by the quaint village name, the description of Sahn Kay Gawk is equally compelling because its worth in terms of labor is established. The focus on assets continues as the labor becomes converted into commodities and commerce. After working as a sewing-machine apprentice, Father becomes a merchant and opens a dry-goods business. As it flourishes, Lowe notes, "A new economic activity was born. Forty years later some of the kinsmen whom Father originally apprenticed were operating their own chain variety dry-goods stores. Numbering more than one hundred, they can be found in every large city from San Diego to Seattle, and as far east as Kansas City, with buying branches even in New York City" (8). The threat of invading yellow hordes is replaced here by the ever-increasing expansion of capital, specifically located within a "new economic activity." While this development does not seem to differ widely from the "old" economic activity, Lowe's characterization of newness suggests both a separation from previous forms of economy that both excluded and exploited Chinese labor, but also that a "new" community has been created.

It is through capital that Lowe imagines a larger community, one based on the exchange of products and monies. Not simply a dry-goods store, it also functions as a bank and place to receive remittances and to send money orders to China. Once again, Lowe details the geographic expanse and diversity of his father's business:

> Thousands of kinsmen and district members, whether farmers, laborers or businessmen, would send their monthly remittances to Father's store. These remittances came from many far-off places in the Western Hemisphere. The checks and drafts that he received from Fairbanks, Alaska; Santiago, Chile; Boston, Massachusetts; Pernambuco, Brazil; and midway points, were in turn transferred into shiny, brand-new twenty-dollar gold pieces, cased in very heavy boxes, and transported on steamers to China. (99–100)

The "brand-new twenty-dollar gold pieces" echo Lowe's earlier claims of a "new economic activity," and we see again the seeming creation, rather than the recirculation, of money. Equally importantly, Lowe demonstrates that the flows of money become the primary means by which community, home, and place—in other words, Chinatown itself—can be established.

> Sun Loy was more than just a bank or a post office, or a store. It was a temporary home to our kinsmen where they gathered nightly to seek escape from the strangeness and fierceness of their everyday world, and could recall happier days at home when they crowded the village inns and ancestral temples of Heong-Sahn at noon and nightfall to drink tea and exchange gossip, or to listen to vagrant minstrels chant ballads of the glories of the "Sahm Kwok." (98)

The economic connections to China translate here into cultural ones, and Lowe describes a process by which the economic and social means of binding community are intertwined and interdependent. For his business partners and employees, he depends on geographical connections from China to ensure the success of the relationship. "His business partners at Sun Loy, for instance, were all from the same village of the same district, Sahn Kay Gawk. . . . When no disagreements intervened, this arrangement, Father explained, produced unity, economy, profits, and social effectiveness" (73). The combination of these terms speaks to the wholeness that is evidenced throughout the book, a wholeness that is achieved through the joining of "economy" and "profits" to "unity" and "social effectiveness."

Father's character and identity emerge only through his ability to preserve the Chinatown economy. When the value of the remittances is embezzled before they can be transferred to China, Father personally attempts to pay back the money with individual loans and the pawning of Mother's jewelry. When the community continues to entrust him with their remittances, Glorious Descendant announces, "They trusted father. He was happy. To be trusted, Father announced, was more important to him than being wealthy"

(102). Despite Lowe's opposition, "trust" and "wealth" are, however, not mutually exclusive here, and Lowe demonstrates that it is only through the maintenance of wealth that "trust," or means of marking social status and communal bonds, can be created.

What I wish to stress here is not merely that assimilation into the United States is dependent on economic exchange, but that the very assertion of Father's identity, as well as that of the larger community and the geographic limits of Chinatown itself, becomes inextricably linked to the circulation of capital. The exchange of goods, services, and "brand-new twenty-dollar gold pieces" also enables Father to move outside of Chinatown's borders, and he becomes the value that is transported through mainstream America. Money also enables a shift in how the state responds to Chinese Americans. Early in the narrative, Lowe explains that Chinese men are barely tolerated by police officers. "It was nothing in those days . . . to find Chinese strung by their pigtails to lampposts, to be cut down by angry Irish policemen, irritated because they had to perform such menial tasks of rescue" (9). One of the later vignettes demonstrates a different relationship to the police, however; here, Father, who carries ten to twenty thousand dollars in gold with him, is accompanied by the police as he moves from the bank to the Federal Reserve and back to the store. Although he is accustomed to making the journey alone, the police insist on protecting him. Finally persuaded, he accepts the police escort. "Neither he nor I ever outgrew the thrill of our weekly ride free of charge in a bullet-proof squad car exposed to the law's naked and righteous might in the shape of two brawny detectives heavily armed with unsheathed, snub-nosed tommy guns" (105). We see here the ease of travel that Father enjoys, one sanctioned and enabled by the state, and the state's protection of his property and person, rights that the ideal American citizen is guaranteed. The transfer of money and goods enables Father's simultaneous symbolic border crossing—movement that echoes earlier descriptions of multinational traffic of people, culture, and cash.

The assertion of this extensive and geographically diverse economic circulation is the basis for Father's status as a model for

Chinese American identity. The exclusion of Chinese Americans can be overcome, Lowe tells us, through economic exchange—not simply through the creation of Chinese American capitalists (important in different ways), but as a model for and means toward social exchange. If Chinatown is a site through which capital moves freely, Lowe argues that its citizens have the potential of also enjoying a similar freedom of movement.

Father's own appearance also takes on the characteristics of money's fluidity. En route to San Francisco every morning, he blends in with the other white suburban commuters:

> Tall and brawny and queueless, Father resembled an American. And yet he was not. Full lips, deep-set almond eyes, and jet-black hair labeled him every inch a Son of Tang. On the other hand, our fellow Chinese travelers simply did not seem to belong. I could see it every morning when the conductor and the brakeman, without fail, nodded at Father graciously. . . . [T]heir cordial greeting were never given to the others . . . whom they disparagingly called Ah John, Ah Charlie, or Ah Jim. (34)

Although Father is marked racially as Chinese, Glorious Descendant also notes the traits that presumably set him apart from his Chinese counterparts. Lowe takes great pains to distinguish Father from the other Chinese passengers and uses physical characteristics to highlight the stark social ones that are delineated to segregate Chinese Americans. And yet, "The moment the cable car stopped on Grant Avenue and we got off in the very heart of the Chinese community, I realized that Father had become an entirely different person. He was Chinese to the core. It amazed me then, but not now for I realize that Father's ability to handle his biracial social life had always been exceptional" (35). While Lowe problematically uses an indistinguishable mass of Chinese peoples as a backdrop for his father's "individuality," Father's mobility parallels the chameleon-like characteristics of money. His role as the conveyor of capital, the facilitator of exchange, the means to its expansion, the father of a new economic activity, enables his own ease of movement, his own seemingly effortless ability to travel across geographic and social boundaries, to adopt different racial personas.

The circulation of monies thus demarcates and also moves beyond the borders of Chinatown as gold crisscrosses its way around and through the region, defining its society and its connections to China and to other parts of the United States and the world. The base relationship between money and national identity is made even more starkly apparent in Lowe's description of how citizenship is acquired. Identity itself can be purchased in the form of a birth certificate and false biography. "All this material and the doctored birth certificate were sent to the purchaser-relative in China. When it was committed to memory, the alleged person whose identity was established on the birth certificate would take passage to this country" (124). Lowe's matter-of-fact descriptions of the transactions utilize the well-understood and accepted rules for exchange to render palatable the illegality of the operation for his U.S. readers. Although Lowe alternately blames the "dark ways and vain tricks" of Chinese peoples as well as their unfair persecution by tenacious immigration officials as reasons for these transactions, its rationality lies in the tidiness of the transaction. The logic of economic exchange anchors the legitimacy of these arrangements and becomes the primary lens through which Lowe narrates the history of Chinese immigration to the United States, the only allowable narrative given the centrality of race as a means of exclusion.

The need to purchase entry into the United States, of course, unveils the overdetermined relationship between capital and race, and despite Pardee Lowe's establishment of the elaborate circulation of commodities, peoples, and monies, he necessarily reveals that race is a means of exclusion from capital's routes. As Lisa Lowe and others have demonstrated, the contradictions of capital expose the process of racialization that consolidates the U.S. nation-state; and Pardee Lowe's claims of Father's and money's easy movement in and out of Chinatown do not fully mask the revelatory moments in which he is prevented from participating in economic activities (new or old) that lie beyond Chinatown's borders. After deciding to become a future President of the United States, Glorious Descendant discovers a less optimistic reality when he is unable to get a summer job as an office boy. As he makes the rounds to apply in person for the various positions, the recurring rejection causes him to question the terms of employment. "Everywhere I was greeted with perturbation, amusement, pity or irritation—and always with identically the same answer. 'Sorry,' they invariably said, 'the position has just been filled.'. . . I sensed that something was radically, fundamentally wrong. . . . What had Father said? 'American firms do not customarily employ Chinese'" (147). When he sees later that the same positions continue to be advertised, he remembers, "I broke down and wept. For the first time I admitted to myself the cruel truth—I didn't have a 'Chinaman's chance' of becoming President of the United States" (147–148).

What is striking here is that the discrimination that he faces is once again located in the economic realm. His realization that he is excluded from national belonging (the dream of becoming President functions as an ideological means to promote the myth of equality) occurs in conjunction with the prejudice he faces in trying to get a job. Lowe's reading and representation of Chinatown and its relationship to the nation-state suggest that the economic stands as the only means of establishing self and community in these critical years of restricted immigration. Documenting the years of the exclusion act and published only the year it was overturned, *Father and Glorious Descendant* works against previous definitions of Chinese Americans as exploited labor. Instead, Lowe focuses on Father's creation of a "new economic activity," one that defines a "new" community as well. Despite the narrative's buoyant tone, the anxiety of such an investment often emerges as race curtails the economic expansion. Lowe notes, "Like Father, Paternal Uncle Number Two believed that America, in an economic sense at least, was his country" (24). We as readers bear witness here to the full possibilities and limits of what being "American" in an "economic sense" might mean.

The Unpredictable Routes of Money

If Pardee Lowe's and Jade Snow Wong's memoirs use exchange and labor to create and define Chinese American identity and a Chinatown community, then C. Y. Lee's and Virginia Lee's works of fiction reveal that the routes of economic exchange can also be unstable and unpredictable, anxieties that parallel the texts' reservations over the future of Chinese Americans in the United States. Perhaps the most well known of these Chinatown narratives, C. Y. Lee's *The Flower Drum Song* achieved bestselling status in 1957 and was subsequently made into both a Richard Rodgers and Oscar Hammerstein musical in 1959 and a Hollywood film in 1961. Like *Fifth Chinese Daughter* and *Father and Glorious Descendant*, it begins by circumscribing the geographic boundaries of Chinatown. Lee opens, "To the casual tourists, Grant Avenue is Chinatown, just another colorful street in San Francisco; to the overseas Chinese, Grant Avenue is their showcase, their livelihood; to the refugees from the mainland, Grant Avenue is Canton" (3). With the first sentence, Lee offers two opposing perspectives, presumably a "Chinese" and "tourist" one. As Sau-ling Wong points out, the novel's basic premise rests on revealing one group to the other, of playing tour-guide and translator to tourists who receive an unadulterated glimpse into Chinatown (See "Autobiography as Guided Chinatown Tour?" pp. 39–42). The opposition between these spaces is particularly borne out by the contrast between Wang Chi-yang and his son Wang Ta, in other words, by the older generation's reluctance to move geographically or culturally beyond the boundaries of Chinatown and his son's refusal to be restricted by those borders. Wang Chi-yang specifically seems to embody many of the Orientalist character traits that critics find objectionable. His storyline revolves around his refusal to adopt Western dress, use Western banks, or consult with Western doctors. His rejection of the "West" and his demands that his sons learn Confucian precepts and marry Chinese women provide a lens through which to imagine an "authentic" Chinese culture for Lee's readers but also ominously suggest that the assimilation of Chinese peoples into the United States is one not politically determined but individually realized by Chinese peoples themselves. It is against this backdrop that Wang Chi-yang's son Wang Ta emerges as representative of a new generation of Chinese Americans, eager to move outside of Chinatown and unwilling to conform to their parents' seemingly outdated Chinese practices. This apparently easy opposition between "East" and "West," ancient and modern, however, is belied by the narrative's routing of the story through the language of money. Money and characters' (in)ability to earn it, store it, give it, exchange it, or steal it signal the text's anxiety over the position of Chinese Americans not only in relationship to each other but to the larger nation-state.

Wang Chi-yang's "Chinese" attributes seem particularly associated with money and luxury Chinese commodities. His fear of banks, his sumptuous home, his love of Chinese antiques all are identifiers of his difference and "Chinese" culture. At the same time, although his son Wang Ta does not overtly shun money, his move away from Chinese heritage and his Americanization is similarly couched in an indifference to money and upper class status—his desire to take a job as a dishwasher, his marriage to a servant, his aversion to Miss Tung's privileging of money. The anxiety over economic exchange merges with the conflict over cultural values, and Wang Ta's desire to be free of his father's expectations leads to a parallel desire to escape the structures of economic value altogether. C. Y. Lee thus juxtaposes this quintessentially American ideal that one can escape those structures with a relentless association between Chinese culture and luxury commodities and money. As I discuss earlier in my introduction, Wang Chi-yang, or "Old Master Wang" as he is often called, is often preoccupied with money; one of the first conflicts in the book revolves around his reluctance to deposit his money in a bank, and his quaint habit of organizing bills by newness. The untainted quality of money suggests for Lee's readers that the money has not entered circulation, that Wang's preservation of it parallels his own lack of desire to move outside of Chinatown.

The notion of money circulating in a closed community is further emphasized by his refusal to bank it. "[Wang Chi-yang] just couldn't compromise with the idea that one's money should be kept in stranger's hands. . . . Money, in his opinion, was like one's wife; he just couldn't let a stranger keep it for him" (5). Money seems here to be oddly divorced from the presumed purpose—as a means and symbol of exchange. Instead, money as an object is itself coveted, to be possessed for the aesthetic properties, and to be bound to like to a wife. It must again stay within the confines of the family and home, to be *taken out of* the circuits of exchange.

Ultimately, however, Old Master Wang (the oft-mentioned title reminds readers of the tradition and "Confucian" hierarchy from which he emerges) is persuaded by his sister-in-law to put his money in a bank. He deposits 87,700 dollars (carried in a shopping bag) in the bank, and he is given checks to use. The fetishization of the bills is transferred onto the act of making out the check.

> Old Master Wang was determined to learn how to write the numbers up to ten thousand, which was the amount of money he intended to keep in his checking account constantly. He found it a great pleasure writing checks; it seemed to give him great authority and make him feel important; besides, it was gratifying to know that the recipient of the check and the people in the bank had to read his writing. (119)

His importance and authority is defined by the ability to write the numbers in English and the understanding that he has an audience for his writing. Communication is made possible through the words on the check—he writes, the bank teller reads—and the exchange of funds is rendered secondary to an exchange of symbolic meaning.

But as Jean-Joseph Goux reminds us, the two are ultimately connected, and we see that Wang's language is itself circumscribed, enabled through the language of money. Goux notes about check writing that "In both the monetary and grammatological realm, we no longer find a full-fledged (as in gold-money), certain guarantee of stable meaning (value) being circulated, but rather writing about writings with no assignable term or end: an indefinite play of referrals that forever postpones the possibility of an actual value that would not be anything but more writing" ("Cash, Check, or Charge," 120).

The "indefinite play of referrals" has already been suggested by Old Master Wang's relationship to the coins, which have also been stripped of their monetary value and instead been imbued with an alternative means of classification based on time or "newness." The importance of Wang Chi-yang's careful scripting of the check's amount does not lie in what that amount of money can purchase but instead in the art of writing itself and the authenticity that it confers. It becomes a means of communication between himself and the bank's tellers—a form of correspondence that, while liberating to Wang Chi-yang, ultimately is severely limited and limiting.

Wang Chi-yang's son, Wang Ta, rejects this economic and geographic isolation and works instead to establish ties to other peoples and institutions inside and outside of Chinatown. Lee characterizes these bonds, however, again through the language of money, a rhetorical move that exposes the instability of money and the complexities inherent in the establishment of both a Chinatown community and its solid positioning vis-à-vis the larger American nation. While Wang Ta's main goal is to achieve "independence," much of the novel revolves around his search for love. This quest is made even more complicated by the scarcity of women in Chinatown, a result of legislation limiting Chinese women's immigration to the United States. Wang Ta's friend, Chang, characterizes the situation using an economic rhetoric of supply and demand, "I always say that to us the girl situation is just like a grocery store in a year of bad inflation. The few items in the store are so highly priced that they are beyond our reach" (22). Unlike Wang Chi-yang's relationship to money, which avoids any reference to value or purchase power, we see in the novel that the circuits of exchange are all too visible for Wang Ta. The inability to control the rapid circulation of money is particularly visible in Wang Ta's desire of the beautiful Miss Tung. The object of several men's affections, Miss Tung moves easily and quickly between them, granting her favors on the basis of the worth of their gifts and offers of financial assistance. While her overt sexuality initially attracts Wang Ta, her facile appropriation of any and all of her suitors' financial favors ultimately repels him. That women can themselves have economic value, that they can themselves be freely circulated while also maintaining some power over their commodification not only threatens Wang Ta's masculinity but also simultaneously suggests his own submission to the indeterminate flows and value of money.

Wang Ta ironically finds himself in Miss Tung's position when he becomes the object of another woman's affections, the "pock-marked" Miss Chao, who seduces Wang Ta while he is in an alcohol-induced stupor. After their sexual liaison, Wang Ta becomes too embarrassed to take her out in public. Miss Chao accuses him, "'You never want to go out with me any more. It won't cost much to go to a movie. If you need money, I have it.' Wang Ta stiffened. He was hit by the remark as if he were stabbed with a knife" (79–80). Once again the attention to money, the suggestion that the relationship depends on an excess or lack of funds, is taboo to Wang Ta. For Wang Ta and his father, money functions in strikingly similar and yet opposing ways. Throughout much of the novel it operates not as a straightforward method of economic exchange but as a means of distorting relationships, the only vehicle for Wang Chi-yang's ghostly communications and the dominant means of structuring (and thwarting) Wang Ta's attempts to find love.

When Wang Ta finally breaks off the relationship with Miss Chao, his guilt overwhelms him. He advises, "Never owe anybody anything . . . either emotionally or materially. I definitely believe now that I shall be happier if everybody owes me a small debt or a slight apology. When I owe somebody something, the debt seems to move into my mind like a cowbird forces its way into another bird's nest and occupies it, keeping peace, its legal occupant, out of it permanently" (84–85). While Wang Ta's father's use of money is evacuated of its power to constitute relationships, Wang Ta resolves to enter into a relationship only when he is the one to whom things are owed. If social relations are created through exchange, he demands his own agency in the transaction in order to not be the passive recipient, whether of his father's funds, Miss Chao's sexual attention, or Miss Tung's unsubtle demands for cash. His rejection of debt, "emotional" or "material," reveals the contradictory nature of economic exchange as it relates to Chinese Americans in the novel. If money functions as the only way to transcend the borders of

Chinatown and perhaps more accurately "Chineseness," how does one then escape economic exchange as a dominant means of articulating one's identity and relationship to society?

Economic, ethnic, and emotional equilibrium is finally achieved through the figure of May Li, a poor but thrifty Chinese woman who performs traditional and modest Chinese songs for appreciative audiences. Wang Ta meets May Li and hires her and her father to work in the Wang household. Through her labor and her attitudes about money, she embodies the conventional and ideal position usually assigned to immigrants and women. Wang Ta's relationship with May Li is in turn based on a paternalistic attitude by which he introduces her to film, food, and kissing. Unlike Miss Tung and Miss Chao, May Li performs Chineseness, femininity, and economic independence with exact ideological accuracy; and her appearance in turn enables Wang Ta's break from his father's house. The climax of the novel occurs when May Li is accused of stealing—an act that once again violates the economic boundaries on which everyone is presumably agreed. She is, however, quickly found innocent, and the novel ends with Wang Ta's own departure from the house as he declares his intention to marry May Li and open his own business. As Wang Chi-yang faces isolation, he decides to give up his "traditional" beliefs on healing, and with a nostalgic tour of Chinatown, he enters the Westernized hospital.

Lee's conclusion suggests then that the resolution to the quandary of racial and ethnic assimilation must necessarily be grounded in ideal definitions of femininity and in achieving a strict economic balance, a state in which a fair amount of money is earned and excessive amounts are never owed, given, stolen, nor coerced. And yet, the novel as a whole belies the notion that exact equivalences, social or economic, are achievable and instead raises doubts about how minorities may achieve national belonging while also interrogating the realities of equitable economic exchange. Despite the suggestion of economic independence for Wang Ta and notwithstanding Wang Chi-yang's entrance into a "Western" institution, the text is laden with economic and cultural anxiety, excess, and imbalance. Although Wang Chi-yang and Wang Ta have entered into new ventures, spaces, and cultural practices, we are left with the unsettling feeling that the cultural and economic equilibrium that has been achieved is a neither permanent nor complete resolution.

The Slippery Value of Chinatown Commodities

> The windows of the Tai Ming Company displayed the works of the skilled craftsmen of China: potteries, porcelains, lacquer ware, enamelware, and ivories. Silk, satin, and brocade had a place to themselves and a corner of the red silk, undone from its roll, touched a *blanc-de-chine* Goddess of Mercy. (3)

Virginia Lee continues to negotiate the path forged by Jade Snow Wong, Pardee Lowe, and C. Y. Lee by questioning the terms of commodity exchange. Her novel, *The House That Tai-Ming Built* (1963), revolves around four generations of Chinese Americans, and particularly the daughter of the last generation, Lin. In the form of stories to her and her brother, the narrative traces Tai Ming's arrival to California in the 1850s to pan for gold. It then follows his grandchildren and their children in the establishment of the House of Tong, a Chinese antiques store, and the Tai Ming Company, a store that sells Chinese goods. The last half of the novel follows Lin's doomed love affair with white American Scott Hayes. Unable to marry in California because of laws against miscegenation, they are prepared to go to Nevada instead, when she is informed of her brother's death in the Pacific, which ultimately persuades her not to marry Scott. The novel ends with the news that Scott too has been killed in the war.

Questions of money, commodities, and consumption permeate the tragic love story as Lee makes repeatedly visible the crises in exchange that each generation faces in its efforts to negotiate the terms of economic and social equivalence. Commodities certainly exist; it seems difficult though to facilitate their circulation. If *The Flower Drum Song* testifies to circulation running amuck, *The House That Tai Ming Built* documents a slower, more truculent flow of monies, people, and commodities. Tai Ming's departure to the United States in the mid-nineteenth century is juxtaposed with his visit to Canton, where he encounters "Jade Street," as well as "Silk Street, Embroidery Street, Fan Street, Lacquer Street, Goldsmith Street, Porcelain Street, Lantern Street" (24). After witnessing the aesthetic and cultural production that is most familiar to Americans of Chinese artistry, he receives an offer from his uncle to pay for passage to the United States. He imagines the United States to be a natural source for unimagined wealth. "Gold! Gold! Gold! Gold is everywhere there! Floating in the river, tumbling from the hills, beneath the earth, perhaps even pouring from the skies!" (29). Here gold is figured as a natural artifact. Unlike the objects in China, which are the products of history and craftsmanship and labor, the gold in America is naturally produced and can be acquired without labor. The abundance of "gold" is symbolic of nature's bounty, and the commodity is depicted as being outside the boundaries of exchange, even as Marx reminds us that the value of gold depends only on its ability to symbolize exchange. Though it will increase the status of the Chinese who travel there to collect it, gold, however, seems "free" for the taking in the United States. Lee juxtaposes the artistry of Canton with the "natural" richness of the gold in the United States in a way that highlights the history of craftsmanship in China, the worth of the commodities, and the corridors of exchange that flourish there (each product has its own street for commerce). The United States, however, is seen as devoid of people and labor, a prelapsarian, precapitalist site that invites entry.

Tai Ming's arrival in the United States, however, reveals that far from being a society free from exchange, it is instead a nation that severely restricts social and economic traffic with Chinese aliens. Virginia Lee describes the discrimination Chinese Americans face, the painstaking labor that goes into panning for gold, as well as the many restrictions that limit how much gold can be collected: "The Americans and Anglo-Saxon immigrants said there were too many Chinese in the mines and took to killing, robbing and torturing them, and said it *was* justifiable, for while the men with the queues took the gold out of the white man's country they never spent it in the white man's country. In truth the Chinese faithfully paid monthly a heavy foreign miner's tax" (45). Lee sets up here the history of the Tai Ming family, and the beginnings of their immigration to the United States. And although each of the subsequent generations returns to China, often to find wives, visit, or to retire, the basis of their stories begins with Tai Ming's desire for gold and his subsequent narrative of the violence of economic exchange.

Despite this history of persecution, exclusion, and exploitation, grandson, Kiang, attempts to succeed in the United States through an expansion of capital. A senior in the "School of Business Administration" at the "University of California," he hopes to develop the Tai Ming company nationally.

> Kiang, a straight-A student since his freshman year, foresaw the day when his entrance into the Tai Ming Company would transform a small two-man business into a national concern. He would take out papers of incorporation and issue capital stock for sale to the public, the family to retain a majority ownership. . . . Teams of salesmen, both white and Chinese, would travel throughout the forty-eight states and Canada and their progress would be carefully watched by Kiang as he moved the pins that represented them on the huge map that would hang on the wall in place of the deceased ancestors' portraits. Sun's and Fook's present policy of oral agreements with their several wholesale customers would be replaced by written agreements made in triplicate; credit would be allowed only upon satisfactory Dun & Bradstreet reports; the system of the abacus and soft-bound account books would be thrown out and replaced with sleek IBM machines operated by efficient young women, both Chinese and white. (125)

I offer this lengthy quotation in order to demonstrate Lee's emphasis on the multifaceted means of entering national modes of exchange and valuing. The company itself becomes a commodity with value to the public; the salespeople crisscross the nation, offering the products from coast to coast, and a map of their trade routes replaces the history of the family, represented by ancestors' portraits. Other traditional methods of doing business within the community itself (i.e., oral agreements) can no longer depend on the shared language and methods of the community itself, but are replaced by "written agreements made in triplicate." The addition of "triplicate" here suggests not only the caution that underlies the agreement, but again highlights the quantity of exchanges that have been multiplied under Kiang's plan. Everything from salespeople to stocks to agreements to machines increases exponentially. The value of other companies needs to be verified by an external organization, Dun and Bradstreet, and lastly the traditional abacus and books are be replaced by the presumably more impersonal "IBM machine." In every example, Lee highlights the movement of exchange from within San Francisco's Chinatown into the larger national sphere, a movement that necessitates a revaluing and translation of Tai Ming, its products, and its associates along nationally accepted terms.

In a move that reiterates the disjuncture between universal logic of economic exchange and the material histories of Chinese Americans, Kiang ultimately is not able to bring the Tai Ming company into the national sphere. Instead, in order to avoid his mother's attempts to arrange his marriage to a Chinese American woman, he impulsively enlists in the army. He is sent to Japan during World War II and is killed there. What are we to make of this move from economic expansion to patriotic martyrdom, as a means of avoiding an arranged marriage, one of the most familiar tropes signifying Chinese tradition and the regeneration of Chinese family? The rejection of Chinese tradition takes the form of patriotism; in order to avoid joining his body in a marriage symbolizing the privileging of the Chinese family, he instead offers and eventually sacrifices his body to the U.S. military. The choice he makes of nation over community parallels his goals of transforming the Tai Ming Company into a national conglomeration, but instead of entering into the circulation of capital and commodities, he instead can only be imagined as providing service for the nation-state. Lee sets up his decision as a rejection of his parents' wishes and of arranged marriages (he demands to have a choice in who he marries), and that rejection would seem to signal a larger rejection of Chinatown and a desire to join the larger national community. At the same time, Lee also suggests that that belonging cannot be found through the circuits of exchange and commodification, only, perversely, through the sacrifice of self for nation.

The tension between Chinatown and national modes of exchange and valuing is again borne out in antique merchants' efforts to establish their authority to value authentic Chinese antiques. Lee foregrounds the larger American public's ignorance of the value of Chinatown goods when she describes their own efforts to enter into Chinatown modes of exchange. She writes:

> Towering above the natives of the Chinese quarter are the tourists: Middle Westerners looking for dark opium dens and pretty, helpless slave girls, nonexistent now though once they abounded on old Dupont street. . . . Tourists from the New England states, from the deep South, admiring a hand-carved, camphor-wood chest from Canton, settling instead for a ten-cent wooden back scratcher. (95)

Although she begins with their "towering" position above Chinatown residents, Lee's portrayal of "tourists" from New England, the Midwest, and the South revolves around their ignorance of Chinatown manners, foods, and products. Instead of "dark opium dens" and "helpless slave girls," and the poverty, immorality, and degradation that those images conjure, Lee attempts to educate her readers on the disparities between their assumptions and valuing of Chinatown products and those of Chinatown residents. Lee subtly suggests that tourists' preferences for the "ten-cent wooden back scratcher" over the "carved, camphor-wood chest from Canton" reveal their own lower status in Chinatown matters, their own inability to distinguish what is truly considered valuable by Chinese standards and what is sold mainly to satisfy white Americans' incorrect assumptions about "Chinese"commodities.

The lure and pitfalls of asserting Asian commodities is particularly evidenced in Lee's descriptions of the contestations over the value of Chinese antiques. She writes, "Profit was not uppermost in [Uncle] Fook's mind. More than anything, he had established the House of Tong as a means to display some of the great art of China still unknown to many Westerners. All too many were the shops on Grant Avenue, now all operated by Chinese merchants, that carried the inferior items of ceramic dolls, back scratchers, and gaudy porcelain pieces" (145). The project of "educating" Westerners seems to be precisely what Asian American critics have objected to about Lee's and other mid-century Chinese American writers' works. The notion that there is some stable and knowable version of Chinese food, customs, art, and culture, and that that version emphasizes the exotic difference of the Chinese peoples, is one that only reinforces the rigid opposition between "East" and "West."

At the same time, however, the act of enlightening Westerners on the value of Chinese antiques reveals a tension here between establishing oneself as an authority on valuing Chinese products and the inability to come to agreement over the value of those artifacts. In other words, the process of establishing the terms for the economic exchange of those products parallels the process of universalizing and nationalizing Chinese Americans themselves. By rendering themselves as authorities for this value, they also succeed in participating in the process of translating other signifiers of identity—not only do they claim commensurate status (class and otherwise) to white Americans, but they also suggest that they can move outside of Chinatown borders and enter into the flows of exchange with other Americans. Lin imagines at first that she can marry Scott, and then move freely within and outside of Chinatown.

Lee, however, again demonstrates her ambivalence about the efficacy of such exchanges, when her characters are ultimately unable to effect fully the translation of and assimilation into mainstream America. The last section of the novel revolves primarily around Lin and her failed love affair with Scott, a white American. Defying her parents' wishes, she attempts to marry him only to discover California's anti-miscegenation laws. They decide instead to elope in Nevada, but at her departure she receives a telegram informing her of her brother's, Kiang's, death in Japan. Taking it as a sign of the hopelessness of her and Scott's relationship, she decides to stay to support her parents through their grief. The novel ends with Scott's own death in World War II. Lin and Scott's failed relationship thus emphasizes the novel's primary dilemma of how equitable exchange can be accomplished in the United States. Like Kiang's inability to move into the national sphere with the Tai Ming Company as well as Lin's failure to marry Scott, the rhetoric of commodities and art that pervades the entire novel signals the unsuccessful translation of "value" and the nonacceptance of Chinese authorities as the determiners of that value.

The connection between social and economic circulation is particularly highlighted in the following exchange. After deciding to elope with Scott in Nevada, Lin decides to share her plans with Uncle Fook, who has been unable to persuade a customer of the worthlessness of her chosen vase. She recounts his conversation:

> "'So you hear the difference in the ring as I tap the coin; original porcelain here and composition there.' [The customer] refused to believe me and left in great anger. She has upset me, and like a fool, I looked at the vase for no fee. Now tell me, don't you think white people are absolutely abominable? Are they not without shame, these white devil-women? How they take advantage of us Sons of Tong."
>
> On and on Fook ranted. Always, when Lin heard these unfair accusations, this blanket indictment of a whole people for the misdeed of one, she shuddered, and she shuddered all the more when she remembered it was the first time she had ever heard her beloved uncle talk so. (200)

The comparisons are striking here. First, we have the vase which has been cleverly repaired to look whole, an attempt to render something valuable or "authentic" when it has lost that value. Fook's inability to persuade the customer that the vase has been tampered with, and that he looks at the vase for "free," suggests that his own time and expertise has been deemed worthless. What is of particular interest to me here as well, however, is the shift from Fook's outrage to Lin's disappointment at his "blanket indictment of a whole people." His own assessment of whites is one that Lin cannot accept, and Lee falls here into a rhetoric of individualism, by which the differences of each individual render him or her a whole and separate entity. Lin seems to reject the very idea of value here—that differences can be collapsed in such a way that equivalences can be measured and ascertained. We see here a crisis in knowledge and value assessment. Even as Fook and Kiang assume that there exists an agreed-upon standard of valuing Chinese objects and labor, Lee herself counters that desire with Lin's contradictory assumptions that value is to be assessed on a case-by-case basis.

The contradiction between a shared valuing of objects in the act of economic exchange and a unique and independent valuing of individuals sets the stage for the inevitable defeat of Lin and Scott's affair. In love with but unable to marry him, the "tragedy" of their love affair becomes the contradictory position of Chinese Americans under conditions of "value." Despite characters' efforts to disrupt mainstream notions of what is valuable or to discount the question of "value" altogether for humanist and aesthetic claims, the novel's ending—Lin's refusal to leave Chinatown, her decision not to marry Scott, Kiang's and Scott's deaths—reveals the inability of escaping the strict constraints and repercussions of value's logic.

Conclusion

Lin's need to establish value parallels the dynamic present in Jade Snow Wong's *Fifth Chinese Daughter*, Pardee Lowe's *Father and Glorious Descendant*, and C. Y. Lee's *The Flower Drum Song*. Caught between the imperative to make visible exchange, labor, money, and value, and the inability to pinpoint worth exactly or to control the flows of money, these characters repeatedly reveal the anxiety and contradictions inherent in locating Chinese American identity and community in the middle of the twentieth century. Although no longer excluded from immigration, Chinese Americans would not be allowed in large numbers into the United States until 1965, two years after the last of these works, Virginia Lee's *The House That Tai-Ming Built*, was published. While the place of Chinese Americans in the United States seems more assured, their entry under a restrictive quota system leaves them in a tenuous state of citizenship that all of these authors work to negotiate. We see in all of the texts the effort to define Chinese Americans and Chinatown in relationship to the larger nation, to delineate its geographic borders, to describe in ethnographic and often Orientalist detail its residents' appearance, customs, and behavior.

At the same time, the characters seem to establish these boundaries only in a larger effort to move past them, and many of the storylines revolve around characters' attempts—none of which are completed successfully or without significant rupture—to travel outside of Chinatown's borders,. The texts themselves all purport to bridge "East" and "West," and their direct address of white audiences seems to confirm that the narratives' primary purpose is to commodify and exoticize Chinese culture for U.S. consumption. While I agree that the texts themselves are valued by their audiences—and well valued given their often bestselling status—for their "insider's" glimpse into Chinatown, I would also argue that in conjunction with the authors' creation of Chinese culture as capital exists an overall preoccupation with and anxiety about value itself and the establishment of economic exchange as a means of asserting Chinatown vis-à-vis the nation-state. Jade Snow Wong's abstraction and alienation of her own labor, Pardee Lowe's repetitive tracing of the circulation of capital, C. Y. Lee's recurring concerns over the consuming dynamics of exchange, and Virginia Lee's consistent but unsuccessful efforts to enter into national circulation all suggest that the commodification and consumption of Chinese American culture and literature is not as easily understood as we might first think. What these authors demonstrate instead is that even as the rhetoric and logic of economic exchange is a necessary means of establishing the very existence of Chinese American culture and history, the slippery nature of exchange can also serve as a tool for disorientation, displacement, and alienation.

2 The Universality of Exchange

Japanese American Travel Narratives and the Emergence of the Global Citizen

In an essay that captures the fullness and complexity of anti-Japanese sentiment during the 1980s, Pulitzer-prize winning historian Theodore H. White easily links the economic aggression of Japan's trade policies during the eighties to its military aggression during World War II. Characterizing the United States as a nation historically dedicated to fair play and one that was especially generous to a humiliated Japan in the aftermath of their defeat, White argues that Japan has repaid this goodwill by stealing American ingenuity, invading American markets, and erecting strict barriers against American imports. Japan's current economic practices are contrasted with U.S. military attitudes following World War II in a way that distills and translates complex political and economic policies into two moments of exchange, one characterized by extraordinary goodwill and fairness, the other by aggressive territorialism. After the surrender, General Douglas MacArthur, White explains, ordered that food meant for U.S. armies be given to Japanese civilians. He demanded also that Japan promote equality at home and in the workplace. White writes, "MacArthur's directives were cut from the cloth of American good will. Japan (so ran his first directive) must completely emancipate Japanese women; must let workers organize in unions; ban abuse of child labor; abolish secret police.

Further, Japan must reorganize its education system and 'democratize' its industrial system" (19). White's characterization is stark here: After fiercely combating and defeating Japanese aggression, the United States (in the form of Douglas MacArthur) practiced and promoted policies in which those in power gave willingly to those in need.

Forty years later, White notes, exchange between Japan and the United States is neither generous nor equal. The GATT (General Agreement on Tariffs and Trade) principles, in which goods should be allowed to flow "freely," while laudable in intent, did not imagine a scenario in which "nations whose workers were grateful for starvation wages would conquer the markets of countries like America, whose workers demanded the world's highest wages." White's logic is fairly simple here. While the United States as a nation has always promoted fair trade and equal exchange (and often very generously), economic excess in the guise of an Asian willingness for exploitation and even to a certain extent U.S. workers' lofty wage demands (one senses White's pride over this, especially in contrast with Asia's workers' abjection) has threatened not only the proper routes of economic circulation, but more specifically threatens U.S. global dominance. Again in language that echoes throughout the media's coverage of Japan's economic advances in the eighties, White raises the specter of Japanese invasion, not of Pearl Harbor, but of U.S. properties, technologies, and industries. He writes:

> Japanese are beginning to supply venture capital for the seedbeds of American technology, from Silicon Valley in California to Route 128 in Boston. They hover over the Draper Laboratories in Massachusetts—the national laboratories that devise the guidance system of our missiles—and acquire what patents security lets free to the public. In the Los Angeles area alone, the Japanese have installed or acquired 1,500 firms. Their acquisitions in our banking system have grown significantly; contrarywise, Americans are all but excluded from Japanese capital markets.

The vision of Japan "hovering" over scientists working on our missile technology certainly makes clear that conflicts over economic trade threaten nothing less than American national security. White warns, "No nation that thinks of itself as an assembly of consumers can resist Japanese penetration. But a nation that thinks of itself as a community has reason for alarm."

White's essay evidences many of the essentialist descriptions and incendiary rhetoric that was characteristic of mainstream reporting of U.S.–Japan relations during the 1980s. His painting of Japanese people as single-minded and as "superb adapters and producers" and his evoking of the imagery of violence and invasion is typical of the coverage of Japan's economic ascendancy and its purchasing of key U.S. properties. While critics have noted the racist undertones to such reporting and the inevitable implications for Japanese and other Asian Americans when Japan is described as both invading enemy and alien, I am also interested here in the economic logic and assumptions that underlie White's rendering of past and present relations between the United States and Japan. His argument that Japan has violated the terms of free trade both in its restrictions on U.S. imports and in their dependence on cheap labor not only demonstrates his belief in the ideal (if not the reality) of free trade, but also highlights his imagining of international economic and politic relations as made up of multiple but equal and/or equitable exchanges. Commodities should be allowed to move freely, into whatever markets demand them. Instead, in rhetoric that implicitly calls up fears of invading Asian hordes, White explains that U.S. products are not allowed into Japan, while "American markets for Japanese good are not only open but come with an invitation." Products such as radios, televisions, videocassette recorders, calculators, office machinery, and motorcycles (all markets in which White notes that Japan has achieved dominance) and automobiles and electronics (sites where Japan was making alarming gains) are tightly controlled and distributed, in ways that take advantage of the United States' presumably relaxed regulations involving trade and consumer information. What I highlight here is that White's inflammatory essay depends not just on fears of Japanese invasion;

instead it also makes important use of our own assumptions and biases about how commodities should be valued and moved. Japan's economic ascendancy is objectionable not simply because their accomplishments, according to White, were grounded on the United States' efforts to build their economy after World War II, but because Japan refuses to allow the free movement of products and capital. Capital here has once again gone awry, and Japan—which White notes is a "locked and closed civilization"—has effectively "locked and closed" markets and circulation.

Such representations of Japan differ significantly from those offered in two Japanese American travel narratives, which primarily revolve around the journeys that third-generation Japanese Americans or *sansei* make to Japan and other parts of Asia. Lydia Minatoya's *Talking to High Monks in the Snow: An Asian American Odyssey* and David Mura's *Turning Japanese: Memoirs of a Sansei* instead define Japan as a site on which exchange (economic, cultural, symbolic) is made possible. As Asian Americans in the United States, Minatoya and Mura recount scenes of alienation and marginalization, whereby Asian difference is performed in narrow and strictly defined ways. Their travels to Japan, China, Nepal (Minatoya), and the Philippines (Mura), however, offer a means of resolving alienation and achieving wholeness—one predicated on the exchangeability, tangibility, and materiality of objects. Unlike dominant narratives of Japan in the eighties, which revolve around inappropriate traffic into the United States and restricted movement into Japan, Mura's and Minatoya's travel narratives, a genre itself defined by movement, imagine a borderless world, in which objects and people move freely. We can see here the intersections of a variety of discourses—race, transnationalism, and economics—whereby the resolution of racial alienation in the United States is effected through the same rhetoric and logic that encourages the free flow of commodities across national borders. Japanese Americans here embody the freedom of migration and transformation, one that enables escape from the borders of marginalization but at the same time addresses anxieties surrounding U.S.–Japan economic warfare.

The link between Asian America and Asia has undergone serious theoretical revision in recent years. As I have previously summarized, it has become clear that a narrative of Asian American history and culture is incomplete without contextualization within the history of U.S. involvement in Asia. The present realities of global capitalism have also vastly impacted our assumptions regarding strict national borders and thus also any definition of "Asian America" that relies too heavily on an "America" that is easily definable or geographically and culturally contained. In short, it has become impossible to read Asian American culture solely within an "American" framework, not only because Asian American history becomes incomprehensible without a full accounting of U.S. actions in the Philippines, Korea, and Vietnam, but also because the nation as a construct is itself in decline. And yet, it is difficult to ignore the arguments concerning the consequences of too closely aligning, and risking the collapse of, Asian America with Asia. Cautioning against the dangers that the adoption of a global identity poses to the viability of a pan-Asian American political coalition, critics have warned against the facile abandonment of a nationally based contextualization of Asian American studies. They argue that such a renunciation would be accompanied by a corresponding collapse of the boundaries that contain and identify a pan-Asian American coalition.[1] While such critics recognize the need for and reasons behind the growing permeability of boundaries that separate Asia and Asian America, their concerns raise questions about how Asian American cultural critics might effectively read the links between Asian America and Asia in such a way that recognizes the history of U.S. imperialism in Asia, the current realities and effects of global capitalism, *and* the imperative of racial minorities in the United States to claim political and social empowerment within that context, a movement that has necessarily aligned Asian Americans with other Americans and that has rejected the "Asian" label, which has historically signified perpetual foreigner.

Early theorists of Asian American studies recognized the radical politics inherent in asserting that the "roots" of Asian America lay in the history of the United States. Published in 1971, *Roots: An Asian American Reader* brought together literary, academic, political, and historical writings devoted to exploring issues important to the establishment of an Asian American identity, community, and history. In its preface, Franklin Odo explains the title's significance: "Our 'roots' go deep into the history of the United States and they can do much to explain who and what we are and how we became this way" (viii). Despite such assertions, he also questions, "What should be a 'proper' stance toward the inculcation or maintenancy of a cultural heritage? How closely, if at all, and in what ways should Asian Americans relate to Asia?" (x). Narratives like Lydia Minatoya's and David Mura's suggest that Asia, and not the United States, functions as the site for identity formation, resolution, and homecoming. Asia is used as a means of rescuing Asian Americans from the margins of United States politics and culture, a particularly striking departure from the claim that Asian American otherness can only be resolved from the site and structures of disempowerment.

As I demonstrated in the last chapter, many first-generation and early Asian American authors have traditionally produced Asia for their American readers, in their roles as, to use Elaine Kim's phrase, "ambassadors of good will."[2] Typically well educated and members of the middle and upper classes, these authors reiterate the opposition between East/tradition and West/modernization, and work in their writings to enlighten their readers on all things Asian. As Kim notes, however, their work is necessarily mediated by their class position, and their representations of Asia reveal only a narrow view of Asian culture, focusing primarily on "ceremonies and customs of food," and making infrequent mention of their experiences in the United States (*Asian American Literature*, 25). These earlier narratives differ in tone and purpose, however, from those more recently written by Asian American writers who utilize Asia as a means of claiming a more whole self.

For such ethnically diverse authors as Amy Tan, V. S. Naipaul, David Mura, Lydia Minatoya, Wendy Law-Yone, Ameena Meer, Chitra Divakaruni, and Le Ly Hayslip, journeys to and ruminations about Asia have provided the means for self-discovery and healing.

Their narratives are filled with moments of cultural illumination and belonging, and the connections they make to their Asian roots enable them to transcend the marginalization experienced in the United States. Lydia Minatoya's *Talking to High Monks in the Snow* and David Mura's *Turning Japanese: Memoirs of a Sansei* juxtapose experiences in Asia with childhood memories of the United States as well as with the histories of *issei* grandparents and *nisei* parents. In combining their Japanese and Japanese American experiences into a seamless whole, Minatoya and Mura suggest that "Asia" enables resolution of their and their parents' and grandparents' alienation in the United States. The logic of such a move—living in Asia allows for a fuller articulation of Asian American identity—is not immediately clear, however. Although such a connection seems self-evident—Asia is automatically assumed to be a part of U.S.-born Asian Americans' lives—I question how those links are actually effected. In Amy Tan's *The Joy Luck Club*, narrator Jing-Mei Woo explains, "The minute our train leaves the Hong Kong border and enters Shenzhen, China, I feel different. I can feel the skin on my forehead tingling, my blood rushing through a new course, my bones aching with a familiar old pain. And I think, My mother was right. I am becoming Chinese" (306). Jing Mei's "Chineseness," prompted simply by a geographic shift, begs the question of how "Chineseness" (or "Japaneseness") materializes and what it might mean to claim an "Asian" instead of an "Asian American" community.

Such a move transforms Asian Americans from U.S. racial minorities into global citizens, and especially into conduits for improved U.S.–Asia relations. In his essay, "We Are *NOT* the World," George Yúdice demonstrates how muticulturalist rhetoric can easily be translated into a discourse promoting the United States as a microcosm of the world. He argues for an increased awareness of the ways in which our desire for knowledge about Americans of color translates into a desire for increased global influence. Yúdice writes, "It is not enough to denounce U.S. imperialism for we incur our own brand of it when we pretend that a more intimate knowledge of U.S. Latinos, African Americans, and Asian Americans, will give us privileged insights into the diversities that constitute Panama,

Angola, Iraq, Vietnam, indeed, the entire world" (214). The expansion of "Asian American" into "Asian-American," in which the hyphen suggests that Asian Americans are fully both "Asian" and "American," or that they enable exchange and movement from "Asia" to "America," neatly moves Asian Americans from the margins of the United States into the center of global relations.

The process of how "Asianness" is produced, however, becomes more clearly visible when we look closely at the profusion of objects in both memoirs. The exchange of objects and the symbolic nature of objects enable, as I argue in this chapter, Minatoya's and Mura's transcendence of the borders that restrict racial minorities and their transformation into global citizens. Lydia Minatoya's *Talking to High Monks in the Snow* specifically concentrates on gift exchange as means of revising the power relations that have defined her in terms of both gender and race. David Mura's *Turning Japanese*, however, calls into question representation as a whole. Through multiple lists of objects (and authors and images) that constitute the primary style of the memoir, Mura questions the ability of signifiers to represent definitively one meaning, an interrogation that ultimately expands infinitely the label of "Asian American." Unlike Pardee Lowe, C. Y. Lee, Jade Snow Wong, and Virginia Lee, for whom objects enabled a metaphorical (albeit not actual) circulation within the larger U.S. imaginary, the objects in Mura's and Minatoya's travel narratives transcend borders in general—borders of race, gender, nation, and even representation itself—allowing the metamorphosis of "Asian American" into a more universal signifier.

Economic as Cultural Exchange: Lydia Minatoya's *Talking to High Monks in the Snow*

Early in their narratives, Minatoya and Mura each identify the point at which Asia and America first intersect for their families—their grandparents' immigration to the United States—thereby establishing their own personal ties to Japan and their families' histories of alienation, isolation, and exile. Minatoya begins her story with her grandmother's arrival in the United States at the turn of the century, to marry a Japanese man already living in the States. Much younger than her husband and a reader of "all the European, great romantic novels," Minatoya's grandmother falls in love with a Filipino man, who, "courted her by bringing books"—until the scandal eventually sends her back to Japan where she is exiled from parents, husband, and children. Although her sin is ostensibly that of adultery, Minatoya makes clear that the taboo of miscegenation and the spectacle of women's sexuality also compound the transgression. Minatoya diffuses the outrage, however, by retelling the affair in terms of a tragic but innocent love story and demonstrates that her grandmother's worldliness—her interest in European books, in Filipino men, their combination on American soil—has caused her exile.

Doubly displaced, once from her homeland and then again from her adopted country, Minatoya's grandmother exemplifies, Minatoya argues, what can happen when women cross the strict boundaries that define the role of wife. Minatoya reads the story from a feminist point of view, and Minatoya's own journey to Japan symbolically brings herself and her grandmother back to their Japanese family, and succeeds in finding the balance between journeying and stability. Minatoya compares her desire for adventure and change with her grandmother's interest in things non-Japanese. "I am the daughter who has wanted to fly, who has picked the wrong men to love, who has started and stopped careers. In my mother's experience, such behavior leads to loss: to hardship, and exile, and to an early death" (115). When her father suggests that she become a librarian or nurse, her mother fiercely whispers, "Do not listen to those old men. Soar as high as you can. Go as far as you want. *Never* let anyone stop you" (115). Minatoya asks us to consider her foremothers as both traditional and adventurous, moderate and extravagant. She sees the same dichotomy in her own life; in another version of a problematic opposition familiar to Asian American critics, she is caught between tradition (her "Japanese" side) and adventure (becoming "Americanized"), torn between homecoming and endless journeying. In the same way that sexuality is recast into the healing discourse of the maternal, her travels are eventually recast as trips home, whether to her extended family, her history, her international family, or her "true" self.

Minatoya suggests here that crossing national and ethnic borders disrupts patriarchal definitions of womanhood, and in a move reminiscent of Amy Tan's *The Joy Luck Club*, offers her own journey through Asia as a feminist move of resistance. At the same time, however, Minatoya emphasizes the strictness of boundaries, the scarceness of opportunity for transgression, in her deployment of economic exchange. Such transactions, although defined by the exchange of goods, monies, and services, serve primarily to highlight the impermeability of racial categorization. Minatoya repeatedly offers scenes in which she and her family enter into unbalanced monetary exchanges. After her father's arrival in the United States, he works as a servant for a wealthy—and assumably white—family, cooking and cleaning for room and board. When his employer discards a briefcase, Minatoya's father discovers it in the garbage. In relating the experience to his daughter, he makes it clear that, although the briefcase had been thrown away, he still had to ask permission to take it:

> "All day, I waited for my employer. I waited for him to return from work, to fix and drink his martini. I served his dinner and my hands shook with impatience. All the time, my mind was on the briefcase. Finally, with a racing heart, I asked if I could use it for my schoolbooks." Father pauses. "My employer was confused, 'Speak clearly, boy!' he cried. I gestured for him to wait. I raced to the end of the long driveway. The briefcase was still there. When I got back to the parlor, my employer was smoking a Havana cigar. The aroma rose rich and woody. I held up the briefcase. I did not say a word. 'Oh, that,' laughed my employer. 'Just take it. It's yours.'"
>
> Fifty years later, recalling this kindness, my father's eyes mist with tears. (20)

While Minatoya explains that her father's emotion stems from an imagined father-son relationship with his employer, her description of the scene is stark in its opposition of luxury and abjection. As her father's employer drinks a martini and smokes a Havana cigar, her father hurries to the trash can to retrieve what has been casually cast aside. What is compelling about the narrative, however, is Minatoya's father's restructuring of the event. Instead of seeing the exchange as symbolic of the vast difference in social position, he instead reimagines it as a bestowal of gift. In *The Gift: The Form and Reason for Exchange in Archaic Societies*, Marcel Mauss demonstrates that the gift, far from being an exchange that occurs outside of political structures and social implications, is in fact highly indicative of how a society is organized. Minatoya's description of gift, however, relies on earlier and still prevalent assumptions about the gift—that its presentation stands outside of any power relations that exist. By reimagining the exchange as one that stems from good will and fellowship, Minatoya's father effectively rewrites the terms of his and his employer's relationship.

Such revision is evident once again when Minatoya's father, a Ph.D. scientist, discovers near his retirement that he is being paid the same salary as his laboratory assistant. He and his employers agree to adjust his pension to reflect a more appropriate compensation. His daughters, claiming "exploitation" and "racial discrimination," demand he contact the American Civil Liberties Union and that he sue. Minatoya writes, "My father studied his American daughters. He gently smiled. 'Before I could sue, I would have to review my life. I would have to doubt the wisdom of loyalty. I would have to call myself a victim and fill myself with bitterness.' He searched our faces for signs of comprehension. 'I cannot bear so great a loss'" (21). We again have here the refusal to recognize the imbalance of the initial exchange. Instead, Minatoya's father suggests that "loss" occurs only if he identifies himself as "victim" or if he reads the relationship between him and his employer as hierarchical. By describing the exchange as a question of "loyalty" rather than one of gross exploitation, Minatoya's father repeats the dynamic at work with the previous employer; the exchanges he makes are made voluntarily and, like gifts, are symbolic of the friendship and good will between two parties.

Minatoya herself is ambivalent about such a reading. She remembers her family's efforts to purchase a new home, only to be told at each location that lots were no longer available. In another instance, "a strange woman" gives her a penny. Minatoya remembers, "The pain of the penny biting into my palm, the horror of her excited face, the self-disgust when . . . I heard myself whisper, 'Thank you'" (29). The exchanges, Minatoya is fully aware, represent more clearly not just the alien status of the Minatoya family, but the gratitude that is expected when the gift—in reality a marker of Minatoya's abject position—is presented. Exchange, she makes equally clear, is often not permitted, or if it occurs, it then fully reveals the seemingly benign but in actuality insidious ways that racial difference is enacted. And she acknowledges (even if her father does not) that within the exchange of each of these "gifts"—a briefcase, a salary, or a penny—lies a social/racial hierarchy that traps and prevents her from, as her mother exhorts her, soaring as high as she can.

The inability to cross racial boundaries is emphasized further with Minatoya's use of performance as a means of social adaptation. Like the economic exchanges that serve only to highlight racial difference even if they can be disguised as mutual admiration, Minatoya's various attempts at assimilation, through performances of gender, religious affinity, and professionalization, only make racial difference even more visible. She writes, "The Japanese know full well the dangers of conspicuousness. 'The nail that sticks out gets pounded down,' cautions an old maxim. In America, Relocation was all the proof they needed" (31). In an effort to be inconspicuous herself, Minatoya quickly understands the value of performance and role playing, learning to give answers that conform to unspoken expectations. When asked in elementary school about her religion, of which she is not sure, she nervously identifies as Christian, and then when pressed, she answers more specifically Protestant, and later even more specifically Methodist, even though her family is in reality unaffiliated religiously. "The children relaxed. 'Me too,' smiled one. 'I'm a Methodist too!' I grinned. I knew that I had passed" (30). Despite her satisfaction at her acceptance and her hope that her performances can transcend her racial features, her accounts demonstrate that the coin of the realm—is she Methodist, Baptist, Catholic?—is difficult to acquire. The social, cultural, and economic exchanges that Minatoya recounts are consistently haunted by the specter of failed exchange, in which equivalence cannot be located.

"Passing" only becomes more complicated as she grows older. When she loses her job, her friends commiserate and encourage her to action. She willingly takes on the roles of job-seeker and academician in her efforts to fit into a social and traditional framework. Her performance seems even natural in its context; she is fulfilling the terms of her contractual relationship with her audience and community. In an obvious play on words, Minatoya describes a friend's advice on "acting": "'Acting starts with just that,' he said patiently. 'Action. . . . One intention, one action, then another, and another, and gradually you are asserting your vision. Your audience—the people who are around you—can recognize and respond to something solid and authentic" (69). Minatoya here implicitly critiques the social exchanges into which Asian Americans are expected to enter. The "action" that they are supposed to offer first is not as transparent as her friend suggests, and the transformation from "acting" to "authenticity" is equally mystifying. That the end product is "authentic" only obscures the manufacturing process at work here, and Minatoya's achievement of exchange with her "audience" is as suspect as her assimilation in elementary school and her father's agreements with his employers. In all of these cases, and through much of Minatoya's family's experiences in the United States, Minatoya exposes the fragile (and often disadvantageous) terms on which equivalence and exchange are achieved.

The exchange relationship that is so fraught as an Asian American in the United States is resolved upon going abroad. In a reversal of Thomas White's essay about the impossibility of economic exchange between the United States and Japan, Minatoya suggests instead (and of course problematically) that for Asian Americans, exchange—cultural and economic—in Asia occurs fluidly and without restriction. Although many of the exchanges that take place in Asia are not without anxiety and confusion, Minatoya suggests that they ultimately achieve a certain purity and transparency, devoid of the racial differentiation that marks exchange within the United States. Minatoya repeatedly offers gift exchange in particular, not as a sign of the social structures and hierarchies, but instead as markers of generosity and good will. Minatoya argues that the boundaries that so fixedly determine her performance of race and gender in the United States, largely fall away in Japan, China, and Nepal, and that she can finally (and easily) follow her mother's exhortations and her grandmother's example of border crossing.

The taxi driver in Japan, upon finding out that she is traveling alone, "turns off the meter and tours [her] around the town" (128). He introduces her to bilingual shopkeepers, teaches her how to catch a train, shows her the post office. When she thanks him with a deep bow, he "shakes his head in vigorous denial of the need for thanks. 'Bye-bye!' he brightly calls. He gives an American wave" (128). Likening him to a "Japanese uncle," Minatoya depicts the relationship not as one of exchange but of gift-giving. She is prevented from proffering money or even thanks, and her role as recipient, unlike that in the exchange in which the white woman gives her the penny and asks, "And what do you say?" does not, Minatoya argues, demand a performance of identity. Similarly, Minatoya's teachers in Japanese language and culture invite her to their home, and during their discussion of research interests, her teachers ask Minatoya if she would like to bring home a stack of books. Although Minatoya assumes that she will only be borrowing the books, when she gets them home, she finds, "Inscribed in the flyleaf of each book is my name, the date, and their signatures" (151). Minatoya's description of herself as the unknowing recipient of a one-way gift exchange enables a reconstruction of self, one that stands outside of expectations or previous constructions of identity.

Minatoya travels next to China to teach "American language and culture," and her students go on a field trip to the supermarket. Although the market is primitive in its technology and depleted of supplies, the students stand in awe. At its exit stands an antiquated cash register. Minatoya writes, "To me it was a relic, a model I had seen in museums of industry. But to my students—jet aircraft engineers who had never seen the interior of an automobile—it was completely captivating." Her students exclaim, "'Within this machine, writing out the bill of purchase, is another wheel in our march toward *upward mobility*'" (179). The class mobility that Minatoya's students exclaim over seems, like the previous exchanges of goods and services, depoliticized, and the supermarket as a primary site for such exchange is in reality barely able to fulfill its purpose. Minatoya here romanticizes primitive exchange, imagining it as the only form of exchange occurring in third-world countries, and in so doing, suggests that in Asia, we might find relationships that prefigure those that are overly determined in the United States. Exchange here is seen as devoid of exploitation, of power struggle, and of hierarchy, and her students' inability to participate in that exchange enables an innocence and authenticity that is unavailable in the United States.

That logic is made particularly clear in Nepal. As Minatoya moves into countries like Nepal, she leaves the roles of ethnic American, dutiful Japanese granddaughter, perky American instructor and settles into a more "natural" basic understanding. In the absence of expectations, she can—and this is perhaps the moral of her narrative—act true to herself. She marks the different pace and values, the increased importance of "life" since it becomes more unpredictable, less controllable than it seems in America, Japan, or even China. In describing her friend and tour guide Pam, who lives in Nepal, Lydia writes, "She has an intimacy with the exhaustion of sudden illness, the sweetness of faith, the inevitability of early death, the tribute of trust" (206–207). Minatoya's imaginings of the simplicity of the Nepali people—the gregarious shopkeeper, the respected military veteran, the innocent young women, the eager children—also succeed in accomplishing a parallel discovery within herself of her own roots. The complexity of her identity and belonging dissolve in a universal simplicity; and in her journeying, she creates a global community that fuses together again the fragments of not only her identity but of the world at large. "For everywhere I went there was goodness—in my students, my travels, my world. Time after time, there it was again: in courage and generosity, in wonder and simplicity, in a genuine gladness of heart" (263).

Economic exchange in Nepal effects the full reversal of the alienating exchange found in the United States. Traveling in Katmandhu, one of her companions spies a shirt on display at a stall. "It was unevenly bleached from too much and too varied exposure to the sun. It was worn along the shoulders from too many years on the hanger. It was missing buttons and was speckled with bird droppings" (240). Although the shirt was not meant for sale, her friend Hank expresses his desire for it. While at first the shopkeeper tries to correct his customer's mistake, he soon gets into the spirit of Hank's performance. Hank models the shirt, admires it, and teases the shopkeeper about the excrement dotting the clothing, while the shopkeeper, his wife, and their children giggle over his appearance. At the end of good-natured kidding on both sides, Hank buys the shirt. Minatoya writes, "[Hank] paid for the shirt. Everyone shook hands with everyone else. Wearing his new purchase, Hank strode manfully into the night. He carried a small paper bag. As a trophy of sportsmanship, the shopkeeper presented him with the international symbol of fine tailoring: extra buttons" (242). The exchange here is a performance of equivalence, even as both parties understand that Hank is receiving a defective product. Unlike exchange in the United States in which exchange enables the reinforcement of rigid racial hierarchies, Minatoya's description of exchange in Nepal attempts the reversal of those hierarchies. In this case, it is the racialized other who has gotten the better bargain in a transaction in which the cultural exchange of a shared joke supersedes the economic loss taken.

The depoliticization of exchange enables Minatoya's own reconstruction of identity and her discovery of her more "authentic" self. She sees parallels between her own identity conflict mediating between East and West and the situations of alienated and fragmented second- and third-world nations such as China and Nepal, caught between their own Asian traditions and the modernization of the West. Minatoya's travels become symbolic of a variety of other journeys that incorporate desire and ultimately the death of home, family, and self—the westernization of Asia, the exile of Minatoya's grandmother, and the writing of her autobiographical narrative. She moves through Asia from Japan to China and then Nepal, where she discovers the prelapsarian world that modern travelers have despaired of ever finding again.

> I am traveling with a face that could belong to a Nepali tribeswoman, through a corridor having its first contact with an outside world. It is a world about which Nepal feels ambivalent. This new world is beckoning. . . . Perhaps I am the personification of barely conscious doubts. . . . I am who the Nepali people may become, and they console me for losses they will sustain. (216)

The quick collapse of historical, political, economic, and cultural differences between Minatoya, an upper middle-class Japanese American woman, and the "Nepali people" tells us much about how easily Asian Americans are imagined in the role of translator between the United States and (all of) Asia. Minatoya here locates herself in the future of Nepal, as the embodiment of a combination of both East and West, primitivism and technology, alien and familiar. Her travels make a series of symbolic connections: East meets West, past meets present, and culture meets essence. Such an understanding confirms the prevailing attitude toward Asia of being both ancient and virginal, while echoing current understandings of Asia as a continent on the move, on its way to becoming industrialized, a fate as natural as Minatoya's own Americanization.

Although exchange is figured as a threat here, Minatoya's overall message is that such a melding of East and West is not only inevitable but ultimately positive. Nepal's modernization becomes one of three intersections between Asia and the United States that Minatoya's narrative reconciles, easily collapsing into Minatoya's own struggle as a racialized minority in the United States and her readers' anxieties about their own unfamiliarity with Asia in an ever-shrinking but economically and culturally complex world. Asian Americans thus become a symbolic means of understanding the United States' new relationships with Asia in a global economy, while globalization perversely provides Asian Americans a new framework for reconciling their own alienation and exile.

The circulation of monies and peoples, which becomes comprehensible and rational in Minatoya's reconciliation of "East" and "West," becomes finalized with her descriptions of objects. They in particular demonstrate the ubiquity of alienation and exile and the notion that boundary transgression (in particular the border between East and West) is possible anywhere. She finds herself at home on the American military base in Japan, where she has been hired to teach English. Resolving previous identity conflicts by redefining contradiction as soothing, familiar, and understandable, Minatoya remarks, "I liked my B[achelor] O[fficer's] Q[uarters]: the sagging narrow bed, its worn corduroy bedspread in jack-o'-lantern orange. I bought a hotplate. I emptied the tiny bar refrigerator of a dozen ice cube trays. I restocked it with tofu and milk. I was at home" (136). Minatoya ironically feels at home in her guest quarters. The unfamiliar objects—the orange bedspread, the hotplate, the tiny refrigerator—come together into a coherent whole that makes its own statement about the confluence of strangeness and familiarity. Her alienation in the United States thus translates itself into an ease abroad, and her struggle for place enables her to find one; she finds "home" in travel, the transitory, and in the temporary home.

Even the westernized hotel in Japan seems familiar, another symbiosis of Japan and America:

> Along the highway's edge, facing a long stretch of flightline fencing, my hotel stands in a border area between America and Japan. . . . My hotel is advertised as a businessman's hotel. It is a Western-style hotel promising efficiency and economy. Yet, Japanese innkeeping traditions linger. . . . My hotel is blanketed by bland indoor-outdoor carpeting, as if in reproachful testimony to some contractor's confusion about how to blend Japanese expectations of inviting nature inward with Western expectations of easy maintenance. . . . The hotel seems a bit like me. Pieces of East, pieces of West forming their own odd integrity. (130–131)

The joining of "tradition" and "efficiency," "nature" and "easy maintenance," and ultimately "East" and "West," offer Minatoya an identity that had been previously unavailable to her in the United States. While her easy opposition of characteristics that are "Eastern"—tradition and artistic harmony—and "Western"—economy and ease—only replicates the very categories that she presumably defies, what is more striking is that the transnational self-realization that she as an Asian American achieves occurs through an exchange of commodities and currency between Japan and the United States. Mirroring the experiences of the American businessman in Japan, Minatoya's reconciliation is made possible only through the logic of global capitalism.

"A Welter of Images": David Mura's *Turning Japanese*

Lydia Minatoya's *Talking to High Monks in the Snow* establishes Japanese American identity through a succession of commodity exchanges. Similarly, David Mura's *Turning Japanese* roots his racial and ethnic identity in Japan by deploying an elaborate system of signs and objects. But in his memoir, objects need not be exchanged as a means of effecting social and cultural equivalence; instead, social relations are achieved through the object's ability to symbolize an infinite number of other objects—in other words through its potential, as the title of Mura's memoir suggests, to "turn" into anything else. Mura's own transformation depends on a chain of equivalence of all objects, an endless linking that enables the articulation of one individual identity and its simultaneous universality.

Like Minatoya, Mura's attempts in Asia to recover a connection with his Japanese past are set against the backdrop of a history of U.S. alienation. His memoir moves back and forth between experiences in Japan and memories of his own childhood and imaginings of his family's traumatic negotiation of the internment and post-war return. Mura explicitly claims Japan as a site for the decentering of the United States' Eurocentric history. He writes, "All my aunt's stories somehow meant more in Japan, assumed their place in a past, a culture that was unimaginably different from Susie's Wasp background, her Mayflower ancestors, the seventeenth-century graves in Sandwich, Massachusetts" (200). Japan becomes here a means of countering the United States' Puritan history, its "Wasp background." At the same time, however, the move from national alienation to self-reconciliation is complicated by Mura's questioning of how identity is constructed. To what extent is he actually "Japanese"? In contrast to the seductive appeal that Asia holds for Minatoya, Mura describes his journey to Japan as being the less-attractive alternative to a trip to France. Unlike others who have yearned to explore their cultural roots, Mura experiences more of a curious apathy. "So, when I did win the fellowship, I felt I was going not as an ardent pilgrim, longing to return to the land of his grandparents, but more like a contestant on a quiz show who finds himself winning a trip to Bali or the Bahamas" (9). He admits, however, that upon his arrival in Japan, he quickly assumes an authority over Japanese behavior and culture, despite his initial unfamiliarity and disinterest in the subject. His wife angrily accuses, "You, you act as if you know everything about politeness. I read as much as you, even more, about this country before we came" (23). Revealing the pressure to authenticate his Asian identity, Mura throughout *Turning Japanese* defends Japanese behavior, offers explanations for cultural differences between Japanese and Americans, and discovers connections between himself and other Japanese that validate his previously alienated Japanese American identity, strategies that place him in the contradictory position to his readers of both expert and ingénue.

Being in Japan also offers Mura a means of reassessing American standards of desire and beauty, and a way to reclaim a masculinity that had been previously undermined in the United States. Mura confesses the extent of his Asian American alienation during a scene in which he finds his father's *Playboy* magazines.

> And so, like many other American boys, I discover my sexuality in the presence of a picture. And, like many other

> American boys, I do not think of the color of the woman's skin. Of course, if she were black or brown or yellow... but she is white, her beauty self-evident. I sense somehow that she must be more beautiful than Asian women, more prestigious. But the forbidden quality of sex overpowers any thought of race. (125)

Mura echoes Minatoya's discussion of the tangled relationship between race and gender, and yet, Mura's representation of Asian women differs from Minatoya's attempt at recuperation. While Minatoya's description of her grandmother's transgressive desire enables her own boundary crossings, Mura's desire of white women becomes evidence of his and his father's own dislocated and emasculated status in the United States. In Japan, however, such desire is normalized. "One discovery I made in Japan was that after years of sexual relations with only white women, of knowing I would marry a white woman, of shunning Asian-American women, I suddenly found Japanese women attractive"(148). In a reversal of his and his father's previous privileging of a white standard of beauty, Mura spends his time in Japan celebrating all things Japanese—its women, culture, and literature. His self-consciousness about his reversals, however, reveal the deeper questions underlying such desire: How easily and under what contexts do signs—such as the Japanese body—gain or lose meaning?

In the United States, Mura argues that meaning is writ large on the racialized body. Describing his childhood eczema, which caused him to scratch himself until he bled, he writes, "Perhaps this is crazy, but I sometimes wonder whether this scratching, this seeming desire to scrape away my skin, might somehow have been connected with what the world around us was telling me, silently, about race. Was my condition a way of speaking about what no one in my family ever talked about—the desire to shed the color of our skin?" (122). Instead of reading race as a construction, Mura names it instead as a biological characteristic of his skin. Throughout *Turning Japanese* Mura questions the body's ability to acquire new forms and meanings. To what extent do his Japanese features and body make him "Japanese"? What seems inherent or essential—his "Japaneseness"—in the United States, however, becomes mutable in Japan—Mura's "Japaneseness" seems quite unlike that of the Japanese—and if the alienated body is physically scarred in America, in Japan it shifts, open to interpretation and meaning.

Racially inscribed as Japanese but culturally distinguished as American, the body emerges as a site of violation and the vehicle for transcendence. Mura offers biological differences between Japanese and Europeans, such as Japanese bodies get colder than those of European descent, that Japanese men have smaller bladders. In these distinctions, he finds stability—assurance that race has a biological basis. He, however, remains frustrated that his white American friend possesses a greater endurance and affinity for the complicated maneuvers of Butoh, a Japanese dance. Finally though through art, the body ultimately functions as a means of transcendence, and while dancing, he imagines his body to be a ball of paper uncrumpling, an emerging larva, a kite.

While Minatoya tells a more developmental narrative that moves gradually toward the establishment of a "real" and more "natural" self, Mura's journey moves in the opposite direction, toward simulation and performance. Japan enables him to question the "real" effects of racial alienation in the United States and instead, as in Butoh, to experiment with infinitely shifting forms. For Lydia Minatoya, Asia becomes a way of generating a global family and belonging. As she looks around at the students she has taught, she glows, "I never have known such belonging" (263). Asia stands as mother, daughter, and home for Minatoya and her readers. For Mura, such "belonging" is temporary, easily adopted depending on time and context. If Minatoya "acts" in the United States and finds it alienating, Mura's "acting" in Japan is liberating. When participating in a political protest in Japan during which everyone wears the same uniform, Mura writes, "Becoming part of a tribe of invisible radicals appealed to me. . . . I was playacting, donning a role I could doff as easily as taking off the mask and cap, the sunglasses and hooded windbreaker. I wasn't going to a political protest. I was attending a masquerade" (208). If his Japanese features fix his identity in the United States, he celebrates the chameleon-like nature of his appearance in Japan.

In fact many of Mura's descriptions focus on appearance. He is "surrounded by this grand display of beautiful young men and women whose every detail of appearance seemed calculated, cool, colorful, and correct" (35). His characterizations of Japanese people center primarily on their clothes: the neatness, uniformity, the sense of their being pleasing to the eye. In speaking about his Japanese acquaintances and friends, he directs his attention again to appearances, the surface of culture that replaces its essence. In meeting a Japanese American friend, he reflects, "Walking among the Japanese crowds, we talked in English. But I didn't feel self-conscious as I sometimes did with Susie. Yuri and I both belonged, and did not; we shared a dual privilege. Even our clothing matched; I was also dressed in a black coat, black pants, white shirt" (152). The shared clothing enables them to pass as Japanese and yet identifies them as a smaller group of their own. At the conclusion of his narrative, Mura wonders, "Suddenly I felt relieved, as if a year-long performance was coming to a close. Was that all it was? A performance?" (367). Both Minatoya's and Mura's distinctions between "authenticity" and "performance" reveal what is at stake for Asian Americans in Asia. Eager to escape, erase, or remake the racial alienation that has defined their existence in the United States, they work (in Minatoya's narrative) to locate a "true" identity that is free from cultural context and bias or (in Mura's memoir) to loosen identity from its basis in the "real" altogether and to question it instead (even while acknowledging its material effects) as a series of constructions. What is important to recognize, however, is that each of their narratives depend significantly on how their readers read Asia, and especially how they read China's, Nepal's, and Japan's progress in the narrative of global capitalism. Masao Miyoshi comments, only somewhat tongue-in-cheek, "Japan's packaging and image-making are world renowned, especially in these days of production and reproduction on the global scale. Even Baudrillard might find Japan's devotion to simulacra a little frightening" (16).

Although their styles differ in terms of Minatoya's tendency toward expansion across national boundaries and Mura's toward the infinite replication of images in Japan, Mura also finds comfort in the familiarity of a transnational culture based on the exchange of commodities. Mura's narrative in fact reads as a collection of lists of objects. One of his first descriptions of Japan reads, "Kanji (characters) were everywhere, but so were Roman letters—McDonald's, Mister Donut, Seibu, Hanae Mori, Häagen-Dazs, the Playboy Club, Antonio's, Kinokuniya, Colonel Sanders' Kentucky Fried Chicken" (14). His apartment reflects a bazaar-like quality and quantity of items. "Photographs of Butoh dancers, prints by Utamaro, tacky tourist watercolors and postcards from Tono, Kamakura, Kurama, on the walls. The pottery in the kitchen, cheap, newly bought, rough-hewn with charm. The TV set and washer picked up on the street, the tables from secondhand furniture stores" (179–180). The inexpensiveness of the items, a quality stressed repeatedly by Mura, highlights their casualness and impermanence, even as their collection suggests an importance that is hinted at but remains ultimately unarticulated. The collection speaks to Mura's aesthetic, his commitment to Japanese art and an offhand knowledge that carries over to the reader who has previously been ignorant of names such as Utamaro, Tono, Kamakura, and Kruma. Mura's lists, like Minatoya's narrative, ultimately, however, depend on the object's potential for circulation.

Each of the objects themselves are not necessarily comprehensible; instead their meaning is derived from their being part of the list. "Seibu," by virtue of its proximity to McDonald's, Mister Donut, and the Playboy Club, becomes recognizable as a restaurant. And except for the Butoh dancers, Mura leaves unspoken what the prints, watercolors, and postcards represent—whether scenes, persons, Japanese art—and yet they indicate some indefinite quality of Japan that Mura has managed to capture and preserve. The properties of the collage are inherently unstable and multivalent, continually referring back to their original meanings and yet simultaneously creating a new totality that radiates a series of multiple readings.[3] It is not only the linking of Mura's Japanese American identity to a present and ancestral Japan that binds the elements together, but also the logic of objects itself, that objects circulate and signify. Like the objects, Mura stands as a signifier of things Japanese to his American readers, able to move easily between Japan and the United States.

His representation of Asia and his own identity as a representative of Asia stand alongside the pictures and even television; and the images that he conjures up—and the images that they themselves call upon—reflect a never-ending series that offers readers infinite images of Japan. The instability of knowledge and of identity and the worldliness that such fluidity imparts is particularly at play in Mura's attempts to demonstrate his fleeting and yet profound connections to Asia. Conversations with most of the Japanese that Mura meets focus on cultural figures prominent within art, literature, and philosophy, and soon escalate into a competition to determine who is the most culturally authoritative about both Japanese and Western cultures. Mura also acknowledges the influence and import of both Japanese and Western philosophers by prefacing his chapters with epigraphs from writers as varied as Susan Sontag, Frantz Fanon, S. I. Hayakawa, Monica Sone, Fumiko Enchi, and Michel Foucault. The quotations and the competition to have read the most well-known authors all point to the value of such cultural knowledge. Mura does not, however, expound on the theories or works of the authors that he mentions; instead he lists them in a manner that exemplifies the postmodern dissemination of knowledge. He describes a scene at the apartment of a woman with whom he is casually flirting.

> I admired her bookcase, shelves of Basho, *The Tales of Genji*, *Confessions of a Mask*, *Some Prefer Nettles*, collections of Chinese poetry, a book on clinical linguistics, art books, Sartre, Joyce, Goethe. What was I reading? she asked. My favorite authors? I mentioned Levi Strauss. "*Tristes Tropique*," she said correcting my pronunciation. "Oh that's rather basic. You should read some of the others." Walter Benjamin.

> "Oh that's good." Czeslaw Milosz who, thank God, she didn't know. Edmund Jabes. (144)

Mura's focus on the signs of knowledge, the authors' names, rather than their theories replicates the philosophy of Japanese postmodern theorist Asada Akira, who accepts that one need only absorb fragments of books. Akira writes, "You don't have to read the whole thing from cover to cover—I think it's all right just to put it by your pillow" (Ivy, 422). This attitude is reproduced not only in the lists of authors that are traded between Mura and his friends, but also between Mura and his readers. The fragments that he offers about Japan and himself do not provide complete histories of either himself or Japan. Instead, the compilation of stories about American expatriates, Mura's father and grandfather, and scenes from Japan's cities and countryside, like the names of the authors, function as objects to be appreciated and assimilated, but are also unmoored from any grounding in time or space. Their endless circulation becomes a postmodern mirror for Mura's own movement and mutability, a circuit of identity formation and reformation that seemingly defies national boundaries and histories.

The melding of history making and the circulation of commodities becomes particularly evident in his efforts to locate his grandparents' beginnings in Japan. When he visits the city of their birth and growing up, however, he finds that the buildings are too new and that even the temple, a symbol of tradition and history, has been built too recently to form a bond that will connect him to his ancestors. As Mura leaves, he glimpses a soda machine carrying "Coke, Fanta, Kirin Orange and Kirin Lemon," hardly a poignant image of farewell. He imagines, however, the ghosts of his grandparents standing next to the machine, waving until he moves out of sight. The images of his grandparents superimposed next to the globally familiar soda machine serves to confirm that symbols of Mura's Japanese heritage remain in short supply, while also suggesting that it is the ability of objects to circulate and to operate as empty signifiers that enables the articulation of a Japanese American identity.

Conclusion

Mura sums up the year abroad with his resulting feelings of freedom. "Japan allowed me to see myself, America, and the world from a perspective that was not white American. I do not feel as bound now by my national identity, do not feel that being an American somehow separates me from the rest of the world" (368). He ends his narrative with the birth of his daughter, whose Japanese, English, and Hungarian Jew roots exemplify an even more complex combination of East and West, of past and present. "I would like to think she is a part of a movement taking place everywhere throughout the globe, our small planet spinning along in blue-black space." (372). The universality that ends both authors' narratives is enabled by the confessions that separate and reunite the narrators with their communities. Minatoya ends her narrative with a family reunion, during which the recovery of a photograph of her exiled grandmother serves to bring her grandmother home as well. Moving across boundaries that separate space and time, during which the "East" comes to represent past, present, and future, they perform in roles that enable them to be Japanese and American, cultural authority and marginalized outsider, alien and resident. At the same time, however, it is clear that the "movement taking place everywhere throughout the globe" is not just the circulation of peoples, but is in fact the circulation of objects. Their exchange (in Minatoya's narrative) and exchangeability (in Mura's memoir) enable the authors' transformations.

Mura and Minatoya effectively persuade their audiences of their ability to adapt to either Asian or American contexts. The fragments from their childhoods and from their journeys into Asia create a collage that suggests at the outset a unity of self, nation, and world. And yet the very levers that enable their entry into and their ability to unite East and West depends on the status of Asia vis-à-vis the United States and their marginalized identity within America. The resolution and ethnic affirmation they discover in Japan and Nepal is predicated equally on the role of industrialization in those countries and on Asian Americans standing as symbols for the shared economic future of Asia and the United States. Their importance as

Asian Americans, and by extension the value of their Asian American narratives, becomes intricately tied to the prominence that Asian first and third worlds hold in the United States' battle to maintain and increase its role as the world's major economic power. In resolving their poignant feelings of alienation by traveling to Asia, Mura and Minatoya simultaneously soothe current anxieties about the United States' ability to maintain its global position and promote a harmonious relationship between Asia and the United States—an alliance all the more possible because of the presumed wholeness that Asian Americans have succeeded in achieving within themselves.

In reading these narratives of loss and eventual discovery of roots and "home," I hope to complicate the ways in which we read Asian America as connected to and representative of the site of Asia in the U.S. consciousness. Such a reading might at first depend on a general skepticism of the inherent authority that Asian Americans have about Asia. Beyond questioning the "truth" of such accounts, I instead argue here that we examine the other links between Asian American and Asia—that is, the circulation of commodities as well as the threats and opportunities that places like Japan and Nepal hold for the United States. Through such an examination, we can see that the question of finding our "roots" in Asia becomes possible only through the dominant and universal languages and logic of economic exchange.

3 The Embodiment of Exchange

Asian Mail-Order Brides, the Threat of Global Capitalism, and the Rescue of the U.S. Nation-State

> American women put themselves on a pedestal and are neglecting U.S. men. . . . It's the same thing as when Ford and General Motors keep turning out bad products. You turn to the Japanese. (Americus Mitchell, Kilmarnock, VA, 67-year-old husband of Maria Victoria Malevo, 21 years old, Quezon City, Philippines—February 5, 1984)
>
> —Raymond A. Joseph, "Wanted in U.S.: Mail-Order Brides"

Americus Mitchell's provocative analogy reveals a great deal about the status of U.S. and Asian women in the global capitalist era. In three brief sentences, he succeeds in drawing on the backlash in the eighties and nineties against U.S. women who work outside the home, as well as on fears of Japan as an economic threat. Speaking specifically about his own decision to marry Ms. Malevo, he also confirms the global capitalist vision of Asian women

This chapter originally was published as "Asian Mail-Order Brides, the Threat of Global Capitalism, and the Rescue of the U.S. Nation-State" in *Feminist Studies*, Volume 32, Number 2 (Summer 2006): 395–419. Reprinted by permission of the publisher, *Feminist Studies*, Inc.

as automatons, while gesturing toward the taboo of the Asian matriarch presiding over the typical American home. Mitchell's comments suggest that a variety of competing value systems are at work here: As white U.S. women continue to "value" themselves more highly, by "putting themselves on a pedestal" and by entering the workforce in greater numbers, U.S. men move outside the nation's borders to locate new domestic and sexual partners. International trade thus becomes intimately linked to a corresponding global community, one in which Asian women might be as easily exchanged/acquired as Asian products. And even as Asian women are imagined to be more firmly located within patriarchal structures, and even as they are represented as being more suited than white women to maintaining "traditional" family values, it becomes clear from Mitchell's statement that the incorporation of Asian mail-order brides into American families reveals the mounting and widespread anxiety surrounding the globalization of the American family and that the linking of Asian women to Asian commodities can be a potent and deeply provoking equation. In this chapter I move from a mapping of narratives that deploy the general logic of economic exchange to an analysis of how the specific rhetoric of capital and profit dominates discussions of the figure of the Asian woman. Particularly pervasive in debates over the mail-order bride, the trauma of capital becomes overwhelming, and we find paradoxically that the mail-order bride's only means of escape lies in transferring herself from the public and global circulation of commodities to laboring within the private and domestic realm.

The number of marriages each year occurring through international matchmaking services is difficult to estimate. In a 1999 report to Congress, the Bureau of Citizenship and Immigration Services noted that they do not require information from applicants regarding their use of an international matchmaking service. They do, however, through surveys by Robert J. Scholes of such companies, estimate the number of these marriages to be between 4,000 and 6,000 in 1998, a number that INS officials confirm as reasonable. Such numbers would suggest that mail-order marriages thus make up between 2.7 and 4.1 percent of female spouse immigration and just 0.4 percent of all immigration to the United States in 1996.[1] The number of mail-order marriages, however, continues to climb. Due to increased numbers of women listed from the former Soviet Union as well as the growth of the industry on the Internet, Scholes estimates the numbers of women listed by international matchmaking services to have risen from 100,000 in 1996 to 150,000 in 1998.[2]

Although the numbers of women who apply for fiancé visas and who are suspected to have used international matchmaking organizations is relatively small in terms of the overall numbers of applications for immigration, the attention paid toward the practice of mail-order marriages has been steadily growing. The business of arranging mail-order marriages alerts us to the intersection of a number of competing global discourses, in which global capitalism has enabled the rearticulation of U.S. patriarchal and imperial desires to "rescue" women from "third-world" poverty and men. Concerned that women in such arrangements are socially and economically dependent on their husbands and fearful that they can easily become victims of domestic abuse without the knowledge and support systems available to effect escape, women's organizations such as GABRIELA Network (working on behalf of Filipinas in the United States) have been agitating U.S. and other governments to halt the traffic of women, and at the very least to regulate the international matchmaking organizations. At the same time, academics have worked to explicate the complex and contradictory political and economic forces that work together to write the body of the mail-order bride; they demonstrate that the industry, especially those companies who work out of Asia, profit from U.S. imperial fantasies about third-world women as well as from global capital's relentless incorporation of third-world women's bodies as labor.[3] Nicole Constable's *Romance on a Global Stage* is a particularly important and recent scholarly contribution to the debates. Through discussions with Filipino–and Chinese–American couples, she complicates the prevailing and static notions of the mail-order bride and offers another means of understanding their experiences besides the often sensationalized portrayals of exploitation. She writes:

> If this study succeeds in its humanistic project of depicting women as something other than mail-order brides, desperate victims, or hyperagents, motivated solely by economic hardship and desperation and willing to marry any western man who approaches them, and if the men (many of them, anyway) can be seen as something other than simply consumers of women as commodities, then this work will have succeeded, at least in part. My aim is to allow the men and women to emerge as a diverse group, with different opinions, experiences, and motivations, and yet to also see them within a particular historical and global context as people who both exert power and are subject to it. (9)

Constable's careful work raises the question that this chapter seeks to address: Why does the language of capital dominate discussions of mail-order brides, and how do we read the use of such rhetoric? I explore here the particular anxiety that mail-order marriages produce and the work that international matchmaking organizations as well as mail-order brides themselves do to assuage that anxiety. While many international matchmaking organizations list women from the former Soviet Union, as well as from Latin America and Africa to a lesser extent, I focus primarily on the rhetoric surrounding Asian women (primarily East and Southeast Asian women are listed by international matchmaking organizations) because of its particular insistence on exploitation and as a means of teasing out the connections between race, gender, and capital in the era of globalization. I explore how the charged and polemic rhetoric surrounding Asian mail-order brides itself reveals a particular crisis regarding third-world women of color within the nuclear American family. The locus of fears about the appearance of global capitalism—and even more simply, money—within the U.S. home, the Asian mail-order bride threatens to unveil not only the economics that structure every marriage but also the specter of exploitation within the U.S.

home itself. A rapidly growing phenomenon of its own, the increased numbers of immigrant women of color taking on the work of caring for U.S. children and cleaning U.S. homes reveals a moment by which the interests of global capital directly confront U.S. ideologies surrounding American families and home-making. While U.S. families participate regularly in the exploitation of third-world women's labor through the consumption of products sewn, assembled, and manufactured by these women, the transfer of that labor directly to the American home has signaled a collision between the needs of capital and U.S. ideologies surrounding home, family, and nation. Often ignoring the economic conditions that make such work necessary, as well as the economic nature of the work itself—simply, that it is in fact paid labor—U.S. families often deploy the rhetoric of "family" as a means of further exploiting the third-world woman's labor; for example, by asking their new "family members" to work longer hours for less compensation.[4]

The need to maintain mutual exclusivity between the discourses of "family" and "capital" becomes increasingly difficult to ensure, as more women all over the world move outside of the home to work, and as more third-world women are hired to work inside U.S. homes. The imperative to preserve that separation becomes even more necessary, however, as the nation-state grows even more dependent on ideologies of "family" to maintain unity and symbolic wholeness. In this chapter, I demonstrate that the figure of the Asian mail-order bride is particularly symbolic of the potential dissolution *and* recovery of a U.S. national identity.[5] Serving as a specter of global capital (and the decline of the nation-state) and as a means by which the United States can reimagine a "traditional" nuclear family within a transnational context, the mail-order bride resonates as a symbol of economic and cultural anxieties surrounding U.S. dominance in the era of globalization. For not only does the Asian mail-order bride signify the labor that enables the "success" of global capitalism, she also becomes a repository for national fears about global competition, loss of U.S. jobs and cultural identity, and the "invasion" of immigrants of color—a threat that becomes particularly palpable when located in the American home.

I focus on three mediums that reflect most cohesively the contradictions among, and even more importantly, the seamless connections between, the predominant competing discourses surrounding the Asian mail-order bride in the transnational era. First, in contemporary U.S. media accounts, the figure of the mail-order bride serves to highlight the contradictions surrounding the processes of global production and consumption. Deployed as a symbol of the danger, seduction, excess, and shame of global capitalism, the mail-order bride links sexuality to economic profit while unmasking the anxiety surrounding the indeterminate process of establishing the value of Asian women's bodies and labor. Second, I discuss the language of the catalogs and Web sites listing Asian women available for international romance. While popular media representations use the Asian mail-order bride to sound the threat of global capitalism to a U.S. national identity, companies that broker international marriages move instead to reiterate the first-world dominance that global capitalism enables. Here Asian women are represented as scarce and underappreciated resources; unable to make a living in their home countries or economically abandoned by "native" men, they are touted as ideal wives, and the logic of global capitalism (i.e., the obvious, efficient, and even moral, necessity of "rescuing her" and transplanting her to the United States) is consistently and implicitly heralded as an effective means by which to reassert U.S. patriarchy and global supremacy.

Last, I investigate the "native informant's" own narrative, Wanwadee Larsen's 1989 memoir, *Confessions of a Mail-Order Bride*, the only published memoir of a contemporary mail-order bride. Here, Larsen, a Thai immigrant, employs the rhetoric of "value" as a means of countering the anxiety of indeterminacy put forward by the media and as a means of resisting the international matchmaking companies' rhetoric of third-world poverty and rescue. Instead, her narrative reestablishes the boundaries between capital and family, demonstrating her abilities to increase her husband's earning potential while also deploying the rhetoric of "family values" as a means of countering the specter of capital that defines mail-order marriages. She thus attempts to move from the position of sexual and domestic worker to universal mother, and her articulation of a transnational culture—one that consists of traditional Asian "values" in an American context—succeeds in assuaging U.S. anxieties surrounding global capitalism, while simultaneously locating Asian women at the center of the entrenched national institution of family. By juxtaposing these three rhetorical strategies, I demonstrate that the figure of the Asian mail-order bride is defined in contradictory yet complementary ways that represent alternately the anxiety surrounding, the promise of, and the resolution to the leviathan of global capitalism.

"He Doesn't Actually 'Buy' His Bride...": Media Representations and the Specter of Asian Women's Domestic and Sexual Labor

The specter of Asian women's labor and its role in the international production of goods and services form the backdrop against which the mail-order bride emerges. While the Asian mail-order bride in the United States is not a new phenomenon—the immigration of "picture brides" was often the means by which Chinese and Japanese bachelors in the late nineteenth and early twentieth centuries found wives—marriages between white men and Asian women, initiated through companies that broker these international meetings, have been facilitated by increasingly rapid modes of economic and cultural exchange between the United States and Asia. The rhetoric surrounding these interactions reveals a larger anxiety over the implications of global capitalism to the U.S. nation-state, and the extent to which national borders can be permeated. Although the entry of Asians into the United States has historically been represented as a threat to U.S. cultural mores, current depictions of Asian mail-order brides seem to evoke specific anxieties surrounding the entry of economic exchange into the realm of the familial.

Media attention on the position of mail-order brides was particularly heightened by the 1995 murder in Seattle of 25-year-old Filipina immigrant Susan Remerata Blackwell by her husband

Timothy Blackwell, after she had initiated divorce proceedings. Portrayed as a tragic example of the dramatic tensions that can result from mail-order marriages, Susan Remerata Blackwell's death was shaped by the media into a familiar narrative that confirmed readers' suspicions about the underlying motives of those who enter into such a relationship. A headline in *The Seattle Times* captures the conflict, "Gunman Felt Duped by Bride From the Start—Wife Alleged Abuse; He Said She Wanted Money, Green Card" (Seven and Haines). Coverage of the murder in *The Seattle Times* provided details of the "poverty" (Henderson) of the Philippines, the amount of money that Blackwell gave Susan Remerata's family ($4,600), the amount of money that Blackwell himself demanded from Remerata for compensation for his total expenses ($17,000), as well as Blackwell's claims of Remerata's repeated requests for money. Echoed throughout media representations of mail-order marriages, the threat of inequality alerts the reader that these relationships should be cause for alarm, not only because of the potential for physical abuse but also because of the economic exchange that marks these relationships.

In coverage of mail-order marriages, reports emphasize numerous ways in which money appears in the process, the economic condition of the women's homelands, the economic prospects of the women themselves, the increased commitment of U.S. women to the workplace, the amount of money the men pay international matchmaking organizations for women's addresses, the amount of money the organizations earn annually, as well as the total amount couples pay for the relationships in travel, communication, and membership to a matchmaking organization. While the economic exploitation in these relationships is a crucial factor of their existence, media representations of mail-order marriages *fixate* on the economics of the relationships, highlighting each transaction, delighting in using economic terms. One article notes "the first listing that comes up in a Web search for 'Mail Order Brides' is 'The Mail Order Bride Warehouse'" (Chang). It adds that "Delaney Davis … is the owner of several Web sites, among them FilipinaWife.com, for those interested in finding a bride from the Philippines. Davis, 60, is not only the seller: he's also a consumer too. A little over a year ago, he married an 18-year-old from the Philippines." And finally, "Owners of these businesses say that what goes on are not cold, commercial transactions: young wives for passports to the first world. They say they encourage real relationships, by stressing the importance of regular communication. [Mike] Krosky [president of Cherry Blossoms], for example, says he offers a money-back satisfaction guarantee—but the client would have to contact at least 100 prospective wives before the money was returned." Terms such as "warehouse," "seller," "consumer," and "money-back satisfaction guarantee" point not only to the existence of economic exchange in the business of mail-order marriages, but also to the taboo that such exchange represents.

Also held up as reason for alarm is the money that permeates the business of arranging mail-order marriages. Another article in *The Seattle Times* notes, "Cherry Blossoms sends the catalog for free but charges $10 per address. A year's subscription that includes 3,000 addresses costs $395. The company grossed $500,000 last year, and takes credit for 10,000 marriages since the business was founded in 1974 by free-wheeling, Harvard-educated John Broussard" (Tizon and Henderson). We see here the media's relentless focus on profit—by grooms, brides, and matchmaking companies—and the assumption that such profit is unique in its reliance on exploitation. In a typically polemical introduction to the subject of mail-order brides in 1989, for example, combative talk-show host Geraldo Rivera titillates by emphasizing exploitation, "Are these [mail-order brides] jumping on the long-distance marital band wagon just to get a passport to the promised land? Or are the American men just marrying these Asian women to get a resident geisha, a household appliance with sex organs, as some critics charge?" (Rivera, 2). Rivera constructs the relationship as a contractual agreement to exchange access to the United States for sexual and domestic labor, an imagined commensurable exchange that is effected through the marriage of an American man to an Asian woman. Marriage functions as the means by which exploitation can take place: either the Asian female succeeds in gaining entry into the

United States without direct approval from the U.S. government, or the U.S. male benefits from unpaid domestic and sexual labor.

Also particularly important is Rivera's mechanization of the Asian woman, naming her "a household appliance with sex organs." Here Rivera not only underscores the value of her sexual labor, but also transforms the Asian woman's body into a machine capable of producing endless product.[6] As the importance of technology and global knowledge has increased, the construction of Asians as technological automatons has become a prevalent means for the United States to represent its fears of Asian economic competition. But the "household appliance's" possession of "sex organs" reiterates the same dismemberment that operates in the employment of Asian female factory workers, while highlighting the feminine in a way that not only defines women solely in terms of their sexuality but also marks the transgressive nature of the exchange and of the female automaton. The image of these technologically transgressive, mechanical Madame Butterflies, produced as if off an assembly line, reveal that the embrace of global capitalism also brings with it profound anxieties over what the resulting transnational culture might look like.

Anxiety over the shifting balance of power between U.S. men (and women) and third-world women (and men) is again revealed in assumptions and accusations that U.S. men are at a disadvantage. In an effort at "balanced" reporting, a report in *The Seattle Times* notes, "On the other side, the male clients who are often ripe to fall in love risk being tricked by women into sending money or being used to gain entry to a First World Country" (Tizon and Henderson). An Ann Landers advice column states their position even more baldly. When a letter writer argues that the best wives are to be found in the Far East, Landers scolds:

> Those "sweet and gentle" young girls from foreign lands who know their place are almost always so desperately poor that marriage to anyone in the United States assures them of a better life than they have. You can be sure that men who marry mail-order brides have been turned down more times than an Army blanket. So get your checkbook out, buster,

> and don't forget to ask for a photo. It's the way to go when you can't compete on an even playing field. ("Women Should Stay in Their Place or They'll Stay Single")

By identifying transnational marriages as being particularly defined by financial and emotional desperation, and by claiming that these "young girls from foreign lands" are "poor," she marks clearly the economic and social status of the women migrating to the United States and implies that their "youth," "foreignness," and "poverty" devalue their status as "wife" in terms of knowledge, culture, and economics. At the same time, the value of the men who seek them is also diminished by the U.S. women who have repeatedly "turned them down." The marriage of these devalued parties results in the males having to financially compensate their brides with money, a means of equalizing their disparate cultural values. Money also serves to make level his inability to "compete on an even playing field" on which he and his U.S. male counterparts are pitted for the acquisition of U.S. women. Landers juxtaposes the cultural equality that the U.S. represents in its "even playing field" with the economic hierarchy that is revealed when women from "foreign lands" or non-European nations are introduced. Thus the valuing and visibility of the Asian woman within the economic sphere—even as her U.S. counterparts remain invisible—exposes the global system of capital threatening the myth of "equality" that defines the U.S. nation-state.

What is striking about the media coverage and popular commentary on mail-order brides is the anxiety over the transgressive link between marriage and economics—in other words, the translation of what has traditionally been valued using the discourse of morality into the language of capital, and the ensuing threat of such an equation to a unified national culture. The predication of the Asian female subject as labor-commodity, however, exposes these systems of production and the new ties in the global era between the moral and economic, connections that suggest that a global culture is necessarily dependent on the shifting definitions and exchanges of value on both the material and cultural levels.[7] By marking these "transactions" as exceptions, media reports suggest that they exist beyond the normal flows of capital, that this manifestation of global capitalism is extreme. Overtly decrying the international trafficking of women as well as the physical and emotional abuse that mail-order brides can experience, media accounts of mail-order marriages also reveal anxiety about global economic exchange, particularly between first-world men and third-world women. In juxtaposing the notion of "real relationships" with "cold, commercial transactions" as Andrew Chang's ABCNews.com article does, his report, as well as others, particularly demonstrates the prevailing mythology that "relationships" (especially romantic ones) exist outside of the "commercial." That distinction becomes particularly crucial in rendering Asian women from countries as varied as China, Thailand, and the Philippines at odds with the typical white middle-class U.S. family, for whom the economic value of labor within the home must always remain hidden. Defined by their labor, third-world poverty, and frantic upward mobility, Asian mail-order brides thus become symbolic of a global economic inequality—one that can be addressed by rendering it an anomaly, separate from other forms of international economic exploitation, and independent of U.S. economic policies and conventional definitions of family.

The Production of Asian Wives

Unlike popular media representations of mail-order brides, which reveal national anxieties about global capitalism through the Asian female body, the companies that broker mail-order marriages seek to assuage such fears through reiterating the global capitalist imperative. Highlighting the naturalness (rather than the mechanization) of Asian women's labor in the home, these organizations suggest that the flows of monies in mail-order marriages are clearly visible and easily traced. Rejecting the fraught ambiguity of the value of a "wife" or a "passport" to the United States, international matchmaking organizations instead concentrate on firmly locating the "female pen pals" (through pictures, descriptions, and addresses) and on making the international marriage process easily comprehensible and feasible for American men (offering trip packages to Asia and legal advice on immigration laws). If mainstream understanding of mail-order brides revolves around the unevenness of the exchange (who is being exploited), then international matchmaking organizations repeatedly signal the opposite, that all forms of exchange (of monies and communication) be clearly defined and definable.

Locating these women discursively—so as to make them more easily consumable—often necessitates, however, a heavy reliance on familiar narratives of race, gender, and imperialism, particularly in discussions of Filipina women. American-Asian Couples, an international matchmaking organization that operated in the early 1990s, confirmed "the Filipina's" familiarity with U.S. culture (and, it goes without saying, did not reveal the history of U.S. imperialism in the Philippines that produced such knowledge) and her innocent and trusting nature. Operating before the proliferation of such companies on the Internet, American-Asian Couples (based in San Jose, California, and advertising their services in such magazines as *Harpers Magazine*) provided, along with photos of available Filipinas, an information sheet, entitled "The Filipina." It notes, "The typical Filipina . . . is petite, feminine, affectionate, traditional, and devoted to her husband. She often looks more Spanish than Asian. She retains the best feminine Asian physical characteristics (small, slender), and personality traits (hard-working, humble, devoted to her husband and family), while being just 'Americanized' enough to be, for the American male, the most desirable mate of all Oriental females." The flyer positions "the Filipina" as physically diminutive and culturally deferential to the U.S. male and suggests that the same qualities ("small," "slender," "hard-working") that presumably render her ideal for manufacturing and assembly work also make her the perfect wife. Her work within the U.S. home connects with her labor in the factory in a move that links the triumph of global capitalism with the resurrection of the U.S. nuclear family.

Reiterating prevailing myths about third-world men's uncontrolled sexuality, American-Asian Couples also portrayed Filipino men as unable to support and care for Filipina women. "Too often, young, eligible Filipino men are too irresponsible. They drink too much, and they chase other women after marriage. Unfortunately employment opportunities are so bad, and wages so low in the Philippines, that even the educated, responsible Filipino men find it very difficult to support a wife or family." In a reminder of the colonial moment, Filipina women are imagined to be in need of rescuing, especially by worldly, older U.S. men. The presumed dependence of Asian women on American men fills a void left by American women as their economic dependence on American men has diminished in the last decades. The value of Asian women thus becomes measured by their need and desire for American men, and as the potential for rescue grows, the more romantic the fairy tale becomes. As Roland Tolentino argues, fantasies of colonialism connect soundly with a nostalgia for the nuclear family in a rhetoric that positions the third-world woman in a domestic sphere that first-world women have presumably abandoned ("Bodies, Letters, Catalogs").

At the same time, the international matchmaking organizations reassure U.S. men that the Asian female—unlike her U.S. counter part—will not follow her first-world sister into economic independence. Once again, the assumptions about the temporal divide between East and West are propped into place, as marriage brokers reassure potential husbands of the traditional values of family and monogamy that their future wives hold. They argue, "They're afraid to leave home and family, but there is simply very little opportunity for a decent, secure life in their country. . . . These young ladies want a man with the characteristics you might have always hoped that someone would appreciate, that is, the fact that you're stable, responsible, loving, gentle, and most of all, *faithful*." The loyalty that Filipina women presumably seek in fact reassures their potential U.S. partners of stability in an era of social and economic flux. While past and current representations of Asian women as sexual and domestic partners for white American men have been primarily configured as a threat to nation and family, the companies brokering the marriages instead advertise Filipina women as already assimilated into American culture and patriarchal structures. Through the U.S. male, the Filipina woman can translate her "natural" tendencies toward feminized labor as well as her devotion to her own family into a commitment to the institution of family in the United States, an allegiance that highlights the universality of family values even as it resurrects the imperial moment of U.S. cultural and economic dominance.

The World Wide Web has greatly facilitated matchmaking companies' efforts, and estimates now put the number of international matchmaking organizations at two hundred.[8] Featuring photographs of Asian women as along with vital statistics such as age, level of education, religion, height, and weight, companies such as Sunshine Girls (appearing on the abovementioned Geraldo Rivera show as well as *Sixty Minutes*), Cherry Blossoms (both of which have been in business for decades), Heart of Asia, and Filipina Lady offer for the price of a "membership" or "subscription" a list of women's addresses. In addition, they sell the means to facilitate a successful relationship, tips on corresponding, translation services, tours to Asia, legal assistance for immigration, and wedding ceremony arrangement. While the international matchmaking organizations on the web often reiterate the language of American-Asian Couples (both Filipina Lady and China Bride promise "traditional" women who possess "family values"), they are also highly interested in managing (and commodifying) every aspect of the journey to marriage. Equally important to the project of defining the Asian mail-order bride culturally and politically is the need to make visible the logic and ease of international cultural and economic exchange.

Heart of Asia (a larger umbrella company for sites such as www.chinabride.com, www.akoreanprincess.com, www.acebubride.com, and www.ajapaneseprincess.com) explains in their "Frequently Asked Questions" section "why . . . so many women from the Philippines [live] in other countries." They write:

> These ladies are hard working and responsible. By going overseas, and even by working as a housekeeper, she can earn much more money than she could in the Philippines. Even college graduates and other professionals often make more money working as housekeepers and domestics than they would back in the Philippines. The money earned usually

goes to support the family left behind, to pay for education of brothers and sisters, and to pay for housing for parents and family.[9]

Not only ignoring the global economic reasons for this migration abroad, this statement also collapses the exploitation of Filipina women's labor with family values and a strong work ethic. The effects of global capitalism only ensure her dedication to her future husband and family, and the flow of monies is made rational. Moving to where her labor ensures the best compensation, she then returns that money back to the Philippines, which will in turn ensure the family's own upward mobility.

While critics of the mail-order bride industry have argued strenuously against the commodification of Asian women, I am particularly interested here in how the language of economic exchange serves not just to objectify Asian women, but how it works to create order out of the chaos that international exchange brings. Cherry Blossoms tells its customers. "Our Travel and Tour Consultants have been helping folks since 1984 and have been to Asia hundreds of times. They know how to help you save time and money and to be very effective towards meeting a beautiful woman for love and marriage. You may find some tours that (seem) to be a bit less, but we can guarantee you that in the long run, our tour is the best value."[10] The rhetoric of value and efficiency here serves to emphasize not only the reputability of the company but also alerts customers that international exchange is inherently stable. Meeting Asian women can be accomplished in conjunction with saving "time and money," a goal that only enhances the upwardly mobile personae of all participants.

The companies also assure potential customers that the money for addresses is well spent. While certainly any business enterprise touts the value of its services, the rhetoric of international matchmaking organizations is particularly striking for its overwhelming and constant reassurance of the existence of economic methodology, the pervasiveness of order. Bridesbymail.com tells its readers, "Most people in the Philippines do not have phones. However, collect calls can quickly get expensive. We suggest you arrange a time where you can call her (you should consider a discount international calling plan), perhaps at a friends [sic] house where they have a phone. We suggest you not give your phone number out until you are ready." And Heart of Asia explains:

> We directly contact the ladies who join our club four to five times each year. If they aren't interested in receiving your letters, they tell us and we remove them from the database. If you purchase an address and she has moved and the letter comes back to you, we give you two other addresses of your choice to compensate. And of course we remove her listing right away. Our records are updated each time we open our mail, so when you place your order, please also choose one or more alternates, just in case one of your initial choices drops out before your order can be processed. We will never sell you an address, if we think there may be a problem with it.

Each of these statements takes great care in detailing a set of precise procedures for communicating with the women listed, but equally importantly explains specifically how that the processes of contacting the women can be managed economically and securely. The painstaking description of how exchange can be effected (either with the women or the international matchmaking organizations) stands in striking contrast to the apprehension that usually surrounds discussions of the immigration of mail-order brides.

Unlike the rhetoric of the mainstream media, value and the means of ascertaining it are rendered determinable and even controllable. Coverage of mail-order brides has focused primarily on money as a means of compensation—that is, money is used to enable women to move out of third-world poverty and money is used to enable men to find partners. And the inability to determine the price for immigration or marriage—or even whether such a price can be set (in other words, name the terms of the exchange)—creates the menace that the media eagerly announces to its readers and viewers. Capital, especially within the global arena, the media seems to suggest, is always threatening to escape the complex series of channels that determine its movement; and the appearance of mail-order brides in the U.S. family stands as one frightening example of capital's pervasiveness even as the immigration of low-waged female labor from Asia, Africa, and Latin America is deemed a more acceptable kind of economic exchange. For international matchmaking organizations, the very indeterminacies that alarm media reporters and their audiences are recast in terms that suggest that all exchange with any of the available women can be clearly defined and completed successfully. Not only are the women themselves knowable and easily situated within familiar narratives of race, gender, and imperialism, but the means of communicating with them, and the finances needed to do so, can also be determined in an equally reassuring fashion. For these organizations and their customers, cultural exchange operates as carefully and efficiently as the circuits of economic production and consumption.

The Rescue of American Family Values

I turn now to the "native" woman herself. Wanwadee Larsen's 1989 memoir *Confessions of a Mail-Order Bride* employs the rhetoric of rescue as a means of transforming the specter of economic exchange into that of a mutually beneficial cultural partnership; however, in her narrative it is the mail-order bride herself who adopts the role of rescuer. Particularly crucial to the telling of Larsen's tale is the articulation of "Asian" values, values that Larsen pointedly heralds as the means of rescuing U.S. men and families from the excesses of U.S. capitalism. As the new wives and mothers of the American family, women from countries like the Philippines and Thailand are recast by Larsen as being valued for their moral and religious principles, a conversion that resituates these women as participating in not economic but cultural exchange. While such a move seemingly rescues mail-order brides from their roles as economic threats and victims, it more accurately demonstrates the fraught positions of Asian immigrant women laborers in the global era. Not only functioning as labor in the production of global capital, their racialized and gendered status as the conveyors of "traditional culture" also places them in the opposing position of saving the first world from the excess and materialism of global capitalism.

Larsen's memoir opens in Thailand with the death of her fiancé, and it continues through to her experiences with an international matchmaker, her immigration to and migration across the United States. As she follows her U.S. husband through a succession of job opportunities, Larsen details her efforts to end his addiction to marijuana. Her campaign to reform her husband enables her to spend much of her narrative as a Thai tour guide, explaining cultural differences between Thailand and the United States especially as they relate to the roles of women as wives and mothers. Larsen's narrative centers around several parallel trajectories of development: her defense of Thai women in the United States as powerful and spiritual; her establishment of the United States as materialistic and excessive; and the Thai woman's innate abilities to reform U.S. men. The juxtaposition of her morality and his immorality within the context of a hypercapitalistic United States works once again to separate the spheres of moral and economic valuing, but Larsen instead uses Asian morality to transform U.S. citizens from their alienated and hypercommodified identities, toward more fulfilling roles as family members and productive citizens. Larsen's focus on Asian spirituality in the face of the United States' fear of Asian technological advancements employs the oft-imagined status of Asia as culturally traditional, even as it reverses the rhetoric surrounding mail-order brides in the current era. Instead of imagining Thai women as economically benefiting from the move to the United States and representing U.S. men and women as their rescuers, Larsen portrays Thai women as the saviors of a morally and spiritually declining nation. Such a shift paradoxically erases the conditions of capital that have defined third-world Asian immigrant women in the era of globalization; by moving the terms of labor from the factory to the home, Larsen also participates in forging a global culture that forgets the logic of late capital. Such amnesia is, of course, highly problematic; however, it demonstrates the imagined and impenetrable barrier between the economic and the cultural that characterizes the position of low-waged Asian immigrant women in the United States. In denying their primary status as machines and workers, these women are thus also seduced into rejecting the economic conditions that define their identities in the United States. Larsen's narrative and other representations of mail-order brides reiterate the status of Asian immigrant women in the global era. Either valued for her "natural" dexterity in the public sphere or her traditional cultural values in the private realm, the Asian woman in the United States enables the nuclear family as well as the U.S. nation-state and global corporation to flourish.

Larsen begins her translation of economic value to cultural value in the prologue, where she writes:

> Yes, far from being "kitchen appliances with sex organs," Asian-American women are as full of questions about life as anyone else. We do indeed have egos, flickering candles capable of flame. If you divide and sub-divide people by race and gender, there is hardly a slice of humanity as diminutive in stature and all-but-invisible as Oriental women. I am not so much complaining as calculating here: as no one else does, the Asian woman acts upon her root belief that in softness and in silence there is enormous strength. (3)

In this passage, we see the strict binaries that she negotiates throughout her narrative—object versus subject, "diminutive" but "strong—and the ways in which she accepts her readers' assumptions only to disrupt them through the language of excess and lack. She asks her readers to consider that the assumed passivity of Asian women is instead a sign of strategy and strength, and from the start of the memoir, she establishes her role as rescuer rather than victim. In stark contrast to the media's characterization of the state of mail-order marriages as one of deficiency and inequality, Larsen describes their marriage as a union between two desirable and upwardly mobile persons. Portraying herself as intelligent, attractive, ambitious, and adventurous, Larsen selects a reputable matchmaker who reportedly deals primarily with persons of the "better class" in

Thailand and the United States. From the six or seven photographs that he shows her, she decides on Richard, the most engaging of the group. She writes, "I studied the picture of an intelligent, handsome face with a smile that in its genuineness seemed enchanting. The eyes were as clear as pools and, according to the information, green in color" (33). Using language typically found in a romance novel, Larsen foreshadows her discovery of the prince in the faraway land. However, she balances her whimsical attitude by noting Richard's potential for class mobility: a Master of Science degree, his interest in computers, and the promise of a steady income. She notes with satisfaction, "The packet of papers before me fairly crackled with *can do*" (33). Combining the attributes of a personal ad and a job application, Larsen's narrative of her search is careful to stress extravagance and surplus rather than necessity and hardship.

Even as Larsen uses the romantic fairy tale as the basis from which this narrative of abundance can depart, she makes sure to let her audience know that *she* also liberates her prince. When she and Richard view the movie *The Thief of Baghdad*, Richard tells her that she looks exactly like the princess of Basra, "whom the prince rescues from Jaffar's foul clutches and eventually marries" (88). She replies that he reminds her of the prince who rescues the princess as he has saved her from a future in Thailand. While the seductiveness of Larsen's *Confessions* hinges on the eventual and conclusive rescue of this "Oriental" damsel in distress, Larsen reverses the story's trajectory by including a reciprocal rescue, in which she pulls Richard back from narrowly being run over by a cab. Shaken up, Richard tells her, "Dee you saved my life." She responds, "It okay. You save mine too. We save each other now" (89). That "exploited," "third-world" "victims" can claim subject status by rescuing "first-world" men demonstrates the contradictory position of "third-world" Asian women with respect to global capitalism. In need of rescue from the effects of global capitalism and at the same time the rescuer of those who profit from these economic exchanges, Larsen and other mail-order brides demonstrate the inability to escape its totalizing effects.

By shifting the emphasis from her third-world status to her traditional Asian morality, Larsen calms Americans' fears about Thai women's presupposed sexuality and greed while highlighting instead their strength and virtue. Moving from "value" to "values," Larsen again elides the importance of economic differences and focuses instead on the power of women to reform men. The immorality that threatens the American family, she tells us, does not come from sources outside of the nation's boundaries, but stems directly from an American obsession with self, as evidenced in Richard's drug use. Drawing on themes that resonated during the Reagan/Bush era, Larsen promotes "American family values" and participates in her own antidrug campaign by persuading her husband that his drug habit limits his American potential for economic advancement and job security. Richard, she tells us "fits the American mold but he also had the 'American disease'" (77). The conflict over Richard's drug use thus symbolizes larger confrontations between traditional Asian values and American first-world excess, and his concluding sobriety testifies to her success and value as an American wife and mother.

As an antidote for America's ills, Larsen holds Thailand up as a model for American reform, and Thai belief in community, stability, and family as a means of countering Americans' pride in their individualism. U.S. children "are among the most unruly in the world" (271), while Thai children, she tells us, are polite, cooperative, and attentive. She argues, "This American husband of mine has apparently embraced too strongly the American ideal of independence; so strongly, in fact, that the meaning has become warped into *defiance*, into *rebellion*—probably a fairly common occurrence in the United States, one that gives rise to the murderous aberrations about which one reads or hears daily in the news" (141). In equating *defiance* and *rebellion*—two quintessentially American themes—with excess and the decline of civilization, she sets up a narrative that places a higher premium on conformity and adherence to societal structures, an attitude that despite its seemingly anti-American and stereotypically "Asian" stance, reassures Americans of Larsen's conservative philosophy.

Larsen further cements her position as America's cultural rehabilitator by outlining the methods that Thai women use to reform men, formulas that assuage U.S. fears about women's empowerment in the United States while simultaneously asserting Thai women's superiority over their U.S. counterparts. Arguing that American women's methods to maintain family ties are too aggressive, she refuses to challenge Richard directly about his drug use, explaining to her readers that "it is not the Oriental way, nor is it *my* way. A hard line stance might bring an immediate foreswearing from him, and grant me a moment's satisfaction, but easily overturned short term results are not what I am after. . . . It will have to be my way, the 'patient Oriental' way or no way at all" (129). Her "patient Oriental" way is a better alternative, Larsen argues, to methods used by U.S. women, and presents a well-known stereotype of Asian women as an effective tool for manipulating U.S. men.

Confronting the charge that Asian women are not as liberated as Western feminists, Larsen muses on the differences between Asian and U.S. women. "To [my mother], a liberated female in the Western sense makes a dozen mistakes and creates a dozen hardships to correct one perceived injustice; and the atmosphere thus created is unhealthy. They score their points but they lose the game" (36). In her efforts to reject the label of a "kitchen appliance with sex organs," Larsen adopts a position traditionally assumed to be held by U.S. women, that of moral guide, a role that is at once humanizing and asexual. In her attempt to rectify the power imbalance between Thailand and the United States, however, she addresses the conflicts between U.S. men and women as well as those between Western feminists and third-world women. By establishing Thai superiority in marriages, parenting, and family values, she enables U.S. readers to envision a global community in which Asian difference and capital is made familiar and less threatening through the gendered politics surrounding motherhood and home.

Larsen thus inverts the statement that Gayatri Chakravorty Spivak so skillfully theorizes in "Can the Subaltern Speak?" in which "White men are saving brown women from brown men" (296). Larsen's actions demonstrate instead that even if that particular rescue is taking place, another is happening simultaneously: "Brown [or yellow] women are saving white men from white women." If Spivak's formulation demonstrates that the subaltern woman is in fact unable to speak, the reversal of its terms does not necessarily signify the achievement of voice. Spivak's analysis is particularly useful in deconstructing the ambivalence and ambiguity of Larsen's efforts to respond to America's presumed premise of individuality and her subsequent attempts to "speak." If the saving of white men does, in fact, discursively move brown women from object to subject status, what does it mean that their only project then becomes to rescue white men? While the white men save brown women from Hindu widow sacrifice, despite the women's "desire" for death, from what fate exactly are white men in Larsen's narrative being saved? Their fears of their declining status as heads of the U.S. nuclear family and larger global community? Larsen's memoir reveals that in the era of global capitalism, Asian women's speech can be defined only through their labor vis-à-vis Western men, while their subject status is dependent on their value as wives—a value determined by their abilities to reiterate and participate in the flows of cultural and economic exchange. Alternately focusing on her Thai and then American sensibilities, Larsen repeatedly resists her Americanization, but ultimately succumbs to it in a move that fulfills the mandate of her rescue by the West, while simultaneously incorporating her own self into the nation as a whole.

The narrative, and the diary entries from which her story stems, for example, conclude only when Larsen is "satisfied that [she had] became a full-fledged American ... [a] citizen of [the] brave new world of freeways, Fourths of July, and fast food" (1). Larsen renders the act of writing dependent on the process of Americanization, an equation that calls into question the relationship of voice and nationality. It confirms U.S. dominant culture's assumptions of the eventuality and rightness of Americanization and reveals that the value of the immigrant's voice lies only in its ability to confirm those ideologies. Undermining her apparent wholesale embrace of American culture and citizenship, however, is her displacement of "America" as a land of redemption and rebirth and her naming of Thailand as a cultural standard. In a final debate over the merits of each culture, Richard points to computers, cigarettes, and automobiles as a sign of American superiority; she counters with Thai tableware, porcelain, and temples. That he focuses on technology while she highlights art again emphasizes the essential dichotomy and irony of Larsen's text: rejecting her reliance on the heightened technology that has facilitated her marriage to Richard, Larsen instead touts Thailand's high culture as a means of asserting her cultural capital, and her beliefs in aesthetic and moral—rather than technological and economic—values, a maneuver that ultimately enables a cultural exchange that masks the material realities of global capitalism. Her ultimate embrace of American culture—her Americanization—she tells us is contingent on a reciprocal American acceptance of Thai culture and values. Eventually, however, Larsen capitulates, and writes the ending familiar to readers of immigrant literature. In the final chapter of her narrative, she admits that life in America *is* better, and in so doing, completes the process of Americanization that she teases throughout the narrative might never happen. The resolution, however, is made ambivalent once again, for in her epilogue, she returns to Thailand and stresses the nation's advancements. For readers who still have lingering doubts about Thailand's third-world status, she makes mention of the new highways, service stations, multi-storied buildings, and shopping centers. Thailand's combination of traditional family values and its adoption of capitalist values mark it as occupying the best of both worlds. Her resistance to U.S. hegemony thus ultimately lies in the construction of a global culture that replicates U.S. economic and cultural values.

The global identity that Larsen constructs becomes a means of integrating not only her alienated self but also unifying a fragmented America. Earlier in the narrative, Larsen remarks:

> Moreover, it will eventually seem to me typically American to have hidden facets to one's personality; this, as a natural consequence of a lack of enduring communities in the United States. . . . In my home town . . . families have been living together for years, decades, centuries even. . . . To some, this

> condition might seem objectionable, but in the Orient we do not have a strong concept of the ego and of the individual's inalienable right to it. (59)

Larsen reinforces the natural association of self, community, and nation, and suggests that the disintegration of the nation produces a simultaneous splintering of the self. Her project then becomes one of reconstituting the wholeness of self, thereby reintegrating the imagined community of nation, and she characterizes Thailand's citizens as the seamless, original, natural self with which Americans have lost touch. "We [Thai] prefer to distinguish ourselves not by being—but by belonging. And we belong not by joining, as is done in the United States, but by simply being. Being in the family, the community—being Siamese" (59). Larsen's naturalization and totalization of the categories of identity and nation confirm the opposition and naturalization of the "first" and "third" worlds, and once again characterize Thailand as a "natural" opposition and precursor to the United States' "constructed" image. However, instead of leaving the cultures as distinct and separate from each other, Larsen uses her family, and her rescue of her husband, to demonstrate the importation of Thai culture into American society. Larsen's repudiation of what she characterizes as Western feminists' dismissal of "third-world women" as "oppressed" becomes the basis of her achievement of American subject status, as she stresses her essential Thai womanhood as a means for reunifying and healing the American family and nation. Maneuvering between the various hegemonic forces under which she lives, Larsen reflects the range of contestations, oppositions, and cooptations that disrupt and enable the overlapping processes of gendered, national, and global consolidation and community-building.

Conclusion

The collapse of Asian, American, and global families into one unit nurtured by an Asian wife/mother ultimately reconciles the rupture between the moral and economic valuing at work in the global era and transforms "the mail-order bride" from sexualized, mechanized, international threat and commodity into traditional homemaker. Employing America's nostalgia for the nuclear family, the continuing backlash against the feminist movement, the anxiety over disintegrating national borders and a fragmented national culture, Larsen suggests that Thai immigrant women can rescue and reconsolidate the U.S. family and nation. By alternating strict contrasts between the United States and Thailand, and trumpeting a united global community—further symbolized by Thai women's status as immigrants and by her biracial child—Larsen positions herself, not as "third-world" victim but as national rescuer.

Such reconciliations and negotiations demonstrate the pitfalls involved in the celebration of transnationalism and alternately multiculturalism, especially when such discourses are used in the re-establishment of the nation-state as model of the world as a whole. While critics have established the limits of nationally or locally based understandings of "culture" (see, for example, Hannerz), I argue that representations of transnational exchanges continue to depend on the gendered and racialized production of culture within a variety of shifting contexts—local, national, and global. Even as Larsen's marriage is produced by increased global capitalist flows, her production of herself as "wife" is largely dependent on her concealment of economic exchange within the realm of cultural exchange, and on her portrayal of Thailand as existing in a primordial, pre–global capitalism state. Larsen's concluding embrace of a combined Thai/American culture serves to uplift U.S. men and U.S. culture as whole, as well as their faith in the American promise of upward mobility even in the global era. It simultaneously demonstrates the links between the creation of a global culture and global capitalism, even as it reveals how increased transnational flows can be utilized simultaneously and contradictorily to erase and resurrect the borders of the nation-state and the citizens and culture that they contain.

In her essay "The Gender and Labor Politics of Postmodernity," Aihwa Ong notes the link between the woman's role in the family and in the factory. She writes:

> In these industries [textiles, apparel, electronics, and footwear], foremen, technicians, supervisors, and labor contractors are almost all men, while shop floor operators and home workers are almost all young women. Thus, the "daughter" status at home is reproduced in the workplace, generating tensions between new feelings of personal freedom on the one hand, and the claims of family and society on the other. (68–69)

Explaining that their work in the factories is often an extension of their expected duties at home, Ong emphasizes that the money these "factory daughters" earn "repa[ys their parents'] gift of life" (69). The connections between labor within a factory and work within the U.S. home are particularly made evident in the rhetoric surrounding Asian mail-order brides. Represented as either symbolic of the threat, excess, and uncontrollability of global capitalism or an example of its logic and the logic of U.S. imperialism, Asian mail-order brides function as a site for expressing both anxiety over and a proposed resolution for global capitalism's inconsistencies. Moreover, as Larsen demonstrates, the only means of escaping this untenable position is to position U.S. men as the victims of global capitalism's fragmenting effects and to name their Asian wives as their rescuers, in effect evading their identification with "third-world" labor and exploitation by fleeing to the U.S. home. Crucial to the creation and maintenance of a global culture, the figure of the Asian mail-order bride stands as a symbol of the cultural exchanges necessary to the reconsolidation of patriarchy and the nation-state in the era of transnationalism. The value of Asian women and their "culture" in the global era thus also lies in their production of "home," one in which the moral and the material merge to contain fears of global capitalism within the seamless integrity of family values, national unity, and global harmony. Asian women thus become an endless source of the potential labor that fulfills the needs of global capitalism and yet saves us from its alienating effects.

4 The Logic of Exchange

Ordering the Chaos of Twentieth-Century Chinese Women's History

A *New York Times* book review of May-lee Chai and Winberg Chai's memoir *The Girl from Purple Mountain: Love, Honor, War, and One Family's Journey from China to America* argues, "If living in interesting times is the curse it's reputed to be, then few people in history have been as accursed as the Chinese in the 20th century. . . . Little wonder, then, that such a turbulent era has inspired so many excellent memoirs" (Krist). The dubious distinction given to the Chinese as the most "accursed" peoples in the modern era marks the nation as symbolic of twentieth-century upheaval, a designation that has been confirmed by the flood of recently published memoirs and novels that work their way through the century's significant political shifts. Written primarily by women—the most notable of which is Jung Chang's *Wild Swans: Three Daughters of China*—the narratives begin with the toppling of the Manchu dynasty and the Japanese occupation of Manchuria and Shanghai and move on to the rise of Mao Tse Tung and the Communist Party. They either then explore the tensions of the Cultural Revolution or trace

An early version of this chapter appeared in "A Woman Is Nothing: Valuing the Modern Chinese Woman's Epic Journey to the West" in East Main Street: Asian American Popular Culture (New York University Press, 2005).

instead their narrators' journeys to the West. Topping bestseller lists in England, Australia, Canada, and the United States, works by the aforementioned Chais, Jung Chang, Leslie Chang, Pang-Mei Natasha Chang, Nien Cheng, and Adeline Yen Mah, as well as novels by Chung Yun Bezine, Lillian Lee, Leslie Li, Bette Bao Lord, and Linda Ching Sledge,[1] although certainly varied in terms of their tone, approach, and stories, all follow the same fundamental trajectory: the women's negotiation of the significant social and political shifts of the twentieth century and the recovery of their stories (often by daughters and granddaughters) at the century's end.

The narratives are striking in their similarities. First, they rely on "History," imagined as a set of objective and agreed-on facts, dates, and political events, to function as another character, an overwhelming series of challenges that generations of Chinese women confront and overcome. Maps, chronologies, and/or extensive family trees all testify to the women's place in Chinese history, a move that argues for our reading of them as authentic and prominent epic figures. The narratives often begin with the early part of the twentieth century as they stress the social changes that occur during the rise of the Republic and of Sun Yat Sen, especially the loosening of social restrictions on women. They take care here to emphasize the merging of "Eastern" and "Western" beliefs and the celebration of modernity, and the heroines of these narratives often stand poised at the edges of time and space. Their narratives are particularly characterized by migration, either across China itself or beyond its borders to Hong Kong, Taiwan, England, and the United States. Secondly, they uniformly focus on several generations of women, highlighting their strength and savvy in the face of great adversity and subordinate social position. Often beginning the story with their diminished status in China—Pang-Mei Natasha Chang's first chapter is entitled "A Woman Is Nothing"—the works then emphasize each woman's rebellion against social restrictions and her heroic efforts to maintain her family's survival in the face of abandonment, isolation, and exile. The heralding of these women's stories (as well as their popularity in the mainstream) suggests that the move of Chinese women from "nothing" to twentieth-century heroine has become an appealing and primary means of imagining Chinese/American women in the global era.

Thirdly, the narratives trace similar economic trajectories, a move that perhaps contributes to their mass popularity. Despite the unpredictable sequence of events that make up the narratives' depictions of history, economic flows enable a linear logic that defines Chinese women as modern and progressive. Their struggle to acquire and distribute capital becomes an important means for establishing their centrality to twentieth-century Chinese history. Either able to succeed despite the interrupted flows of money or because of their power to control its unpredictability, the women in these narratives offer readers a sense that they can maintain stability, family, and security in the midst of political and social upheaval across two continents. The narratives each interrogate the "value" of women, defined first through the transfer of their labor power to their husbands' families. The stories, however, demonstrate that despite assumptions that "a woman is nothing," the women are the primary means of keeping the family intact in the face of national disintegration. Their "nothingness" thus becomes transformed into assets and wealth, a move that parallels the insertion of their stories into an "official" Chinese history.

In this chapter I focus on three of these recently published memoirs: Adeline Yen Mah's *Falling Leaves: The Memoir of an Unwanted Chinese Daughter* (1997), Pang-Mei Natasha Chang's *Bound Feet and Western Dress: A Memoir* (1996), and May-lee Chai and Winberg Chai's *The Girl from Purple Mountain: Love, Honor, War, and One Family's Journey from China to America* (2001). Written by Chinese Americans about either their own or their foremothers' experiences, they are representative of the genre as a whole and particularly make visible the memoirs' central focus on Chinese women's trauma and their abilities to keep their families intact, especially through their steady regulation of the flows of economic circulation. The spectacle of the Chinese woman who resists patriarchal structures while maintaining national and familial traditions becomes particularly resonant when placed against the figure of the diasporic Chinese businessman whose citizenship, as Aihwa Ong makes clear, becomes subject to the demands of global capital. Citing his "flexible citizenship," which "refers to the cultural logics of capitalist accumulation, travel, and displacement that induce subjects to respond fluidly and opportunistically to changing political-economic conditions," Ong explains that "the image of the border-running Chinese executive with no state loyalty has become an important figure in the era of Pacific Rim capital" (Flexible Citizenship, 135–136). Equally pervasive and important at this particular moment, I would argue, is the figure of the persecuted Chinese female expatriate, who emerges victorious and whole from the tumultuous, fragmenting, and dramatic events of the last century.

She also emerges as the means by which monies can be safely hoarded and circulated. If the Chinese businessman abroad has become identified by his mobile ability to accommodate his needs to those of global capitalism, then the Chinese woman in the West, whose mobility responds solely to the shifting political landscape, has instead become the superhuman figure who regulates the economic chaos at home. The inability to locate Chinese diasporic men decisively—since their flexibility demands that capital, not national borders, be the primary coordinates for travel—is countered by a hyperidentification of Chinese women with nation, its history, conflicts, landscape, chronology, past and future, and, equally importantly, its monies.

History as Excess

Adeline Yen Mah's *Falling Leaves: The True Story of an Unwanted Chinese Daughter* especially narrates and argues against the capricious and inequitable distribution of wealth. First published in Great Britain and rising to the bestseller lists there and in Hong Kong, Australia, and the United States, *Falling Leaves* is Mah's memoir of emotional abuse and isolation. Set against the Japanese invasion of China and the rise to power of the Communist rebels, the work charts the warfare within the Yen family itself, specifically centering on money as a means of disenfranchising family members.

Despite being the daughter of a wealthy businessman, Mah's story revolves around lack—of money, attention, affection, support—and her struggle to succeed professionally and to strengthen familial ties. While her story reiterates such liberal humanist values as self-reliance, upward mobility, and ironically enough, the rejection of excessive accumulation of capital, its narrative trajectory from deprivation to abundance parallels the other moves that Mah's memoir makes—its representation of history as progressive and Chinese women's history as particularly triumphant.

The dramatic differences between excess and scarcity are exemplified in the opposition between the two maternal figures in Mah's text. Although Mah's own mother dies shortly after Mah's birth, Mah is raised by her Aunt Baba, a model of self-sacrifice. Mah's stepmother (whom the children call Niang), in turn, is characterized by her extravagant consumption and miserly attitude toward her stepchildren and provides much of the backdrop to Mah's narrative of alienation. These women's relationship to Mah and to each other seems inversely proportional: the less affection Niang bestows upon Mah, the more Aunt Baba acts as her protector; the more money Niang commands, the less Aunt Baba receives; when Niang flees to and thrives in capitalist Hong Kong, Aunt Baba elects to stay in China and has most of her possessions and property stripped from her.

Niang's financial control of the family is particularly emphasized at the story's start and end. Mah begins her memoir with the reading of her father's will. Niang abruptly closes the meeting, stating only that their father had no funds to bequeath. Mah closes her story with Niang's death, and Mah's own disinheritance. Money stands as the literal and symbolic cause of the fragmentation of Mah's family, and its unequal and unpredictable distribution a means of highlighting the instability and violence that surrounds twentieth-century members of the Chinese diaspora.

Chronologically, Mah juxtaposes the rupture of the Yen family with the fragmentation of China as a whole, and the many moves that various family members make to Hong Kong, Canada, Britain, Nigeria, and Southern California replicate the experiences of the wealthiest Chinese elite after the Communist victory. At the same time, however, by intertwining national and familial history, Mah suggests that the struggles for power and belonging within her own family only replicate the larger battles for dominance and unity within China. The interdependence of national events with the personal struggles of one alienated girl reinforces the epic dimensions of Mah's story even as it brings national events into the realm of fairy tales. The blurring of the forms can be seen in the following passage, in which Niang's actions are collapsed with the Japanese invasion of China. One of Niang's first acts is to give her stepchildren English names:

> Overnight, my sister Jun-pei became Lydia, my three brothers Zi-jie, Zi-lin and Zi-jun were named Gregory, Edgar and James, and I, Jun-ling, was called Adeline.
>
> Japanese troops, which already occupied Tianjin and Beijing, were now moving steadily southwards. They met surprisingly strong resistance in Nanking and, in retaliation, went on a terrifying spree of rape, looting and murder. Over 300,000 civilians and prisoners of war were tortured and killed during the Rape of Nanking in 1937 and early 1938 after the city was captured by the Japanese. (30)

"History," although ostensibly used to contextualize the significant moments in Adeline's own story, also serves here to reinforce the traumatic invasion of the Yen family by Niang, and to highlight the chaos and shifts in power that threaten Adeline and divide the family. While the historical "facts"—numbers of victims and dates—authenticate and authorize Mah's narrative, her own story transforms Chinese "history" into a tale of "good" versus "evil," devoid of social, economic, and political considerations. Such a rendition universalizes the twentieth century in China, depicting it as a frenzied, tragic era, filled with famine, displacement, destruction, and death. While such a backdrop of human misery certainly imbues the narratives' heroines with a greater sense of triumph, we must consider why the spectacle of twentieth-century Chinese mass suffering has become such a ubiquitous and powerful symbol.

These images of mass dispersal and destruction work as reminders of the modern era, an epoch of bombs, advanced weaponry and technology, and anguish on a scale previously unheard of. While reading about such trauma may work to reassure middle-class Western readers of the comfort and safety within their own lives, the depictions also effect a vision of history, especially Chinese history, as fated and destined. Beyond people's control, Mah's and others' renditions of floods, famines, invasions, wars, as well as Communist campaigns such as the Great Leap Forward and the Cultural Revolution, all promote "history" as a series of inevitable events to which the narrators and their families have fallen victim. The chaos of the twentieth century, although unimaginable and seemingly unmanageable, can, however, be overcome through individual will and determination. By distilling "300,000" stories into one personal tale of familial betrayal and alienation, Mah transforms the chaos of the modern era into a reiteration of traditional family values. In the face of mass migrations in the current era (and certainly the populations of the People's Republic of China have particularly come to symbolize an enormous and undifferentiated mass for U.S. peoples), Adeline's efforts even more strongly speak to the power of loyalty, family, and the ties that bind one to one's mother and motherland. Arjun Appadurai notes, "The past is now not a land to return to in a simple politics of memory. It has become a synchronic warehouse of cultural scenarios, a kind of temporal central casting, to which recourse can be taken as appropriate, depending on the movie to be made, the scene to be enacted, the hostages to be rescued" (Modernity at Large, 30). Twentieth-century China in *Falling Leaves* and in the other narratives of this genre emerges as the historical backdrop of choice for Western readers in their efforts to grapple with present and postmodern anxieties about global migration and dehumanization. Not only can these concerns be displaced onto another time and place, but *Falling Leaves* and other memoirs reassure us of the universality and individuality that can triumph over these forces of mass dispersal and destruction.

The vulnerability of the Chinese peoples is particularly emphasized with Mah's and other family members' experiences of deprivation as Niang gains more power within the family. Despite the invasion of Japanese forces and the battles between communist and nationalist armies, Mah's father only becomes wealthier, successfully protecting bank accounts and sources of capital from being seized by those (temporarily) in power. When he finally flees China and moves to Hong Kong, he again acquires more wealth. In a passage that is remarkably similar to those written by Chinese American writers fifty years earlier, Mah details her father's economic accomplishments.

> Father quickly adapted to business life in the British colony. First he set up a flourishing import-export company. Then he astutely traded in stocks, commodities and foreign currencies. He launched a property company. . . . He obtained the right to dispose of the loose gravel, stones and earth when Stubbs Road was lengthened. . . . He created a temporary quarry and sold the excavated materials to eager builders. He became a member of many of the most prestigious clubs in Hong Kong and was known as a successful entrepreneur from Shanghai. (97)

Mah juxtaposes this excess with her own experiences of deprivation at the Sacred Heart Convent School and Orphanage in Hong Kong, where her parents enroll her. She explains that the student hierarchy is determined by the amount of attention they receive from home—presents, food, visits. Eggs, she tells us, are particularly prized; girls often receive eggs from home, and they are cooked during breakfast, with each girl accepting her cooked egg only when her name is called. Mah writes, "The breakfast egg, more than anything, divided us into two distinct and transparent groups: the loved ones and the unloved ones. Needless to say, I remained eggless throughout my tenure at Sacred Heart" (101–102). The stark contrast between her parents' wealth and her own lack only underscores the profound ruptures in family and nation.

As the fortunes of her parents are on the rise, Aunt Baba, who has elected to remain in Shanghai, steadily becomes impoverished.

During the Cultural Revolution, Aunt Baba's house is destroyed and she is summarily evicted:

> She was allotted fifteen yuan per month by the government for living expenses and instructed to wear a piece of black cloth on her chest. . . . She was now a despised 'black.' The blacks were the capitalist, landlord, rightest, rich peasant, counter-revolutionary and criminal element. They were given the most menial jobs and were invariably the last to be served in food lines and other queues. (203)

History here becomes easily demarcated by excess and deprivation, by the extremes of rich and poor, the grossness of capitalism, the abjection of communism. The opposition between Hong Kong and China, cultural corruption and national purity, surplus and lack also allows for the production of surplus value itself through the body of the Chinese woman. As Rey Chow explains, "The 'Third World,' as the site of the 'raw' material that is 'monstrosity,' is produced for the surplus-value of spectacle, entertainment, and spiritual enrichment for the 'First World'" (84).[2] It is the "rawness" of deprivation—experienced by Aunt Baba during the cultural revolution and Mah herself at the orphanage—that becomes surplus value, even if Mah herself seems to be arguing that the excesses of capitalism moves one farther from the "essence" of China, stripped of luxuries like "presents" and "visits" and "eggs," and necessities like housing, food, employment, and medical care.

Economic deprivation is thus equated with a longing for family and nation, and the memoir concludes satisfactorily with Mah's return to China and to her Aunt Baba. While her stepmother has once again and finally withheld monies from Mah by leaving her out of her will, Niang's invasion into the Yen family, the dispersal and fragmentation of the Chinese peoples, and the unity of family and nation are all resolved by history's inevitable destination of progress and modernity. The specter of the third-world, global capitalist woman, unmoored from nation and family, is firmly banished when Adeline returns to China to sit at Aunt Baba's deathbed. Mah remembers, "In her modest and unassuming way, [Aunt Baba] had guided me towards a spirit of independence which she herself had manifested by rebuffing Niang and remaining in Shanghai. Aunt Baba was not one to dwell on the bitter hardships she suffered during the Cultural Revolution. Love, generosity and humour never left her" (274).

Further emphasizing the opposition between excessive diasporic hybridity and national cultural purity are the two models of womanhood that Mah offers—Eurasian stepmother Niang and Adeline's Aunt Baba. Descriptions of Niang particularly play up her French and Chinese roots, connecting her mixed heritage to her insatiable desire for grandeur. She writes about her stepmother, "Jeanne's taste reflected her mixed origins. She invariably wore western clothes and she wore them well. She liked to be surrounded by French furniture, red velvet curtains and richly textured wallpaper. At the same time, she collected antique Chinese porcelain, paintings and chairs" (29). Niang's ability to surround herself with aesthetic extravagance and her relentless consumption stand in marked contrast to Aunt Baba, who gives up her own financial and personal desires to act as caretaker to Adeline and her brothers and sisters when their mother dies. In addition, when Niang withholds money from her stepchildren and in-laws as a form of punishment, Aunt Baba uses her meager salary to support her father and to provide a small allowance for Adeline. And her life in China at the end of the twentieth century provides a stark contrast to Niang's lavish lifestyle at its start. "[Aunt Baba's] room was cold and dingy. The only furniture was a bed, a wooden table and one small, hard-backed chair. All her earthly possessions were kept in one large wooden trunk and some cardboard boxes stacked in rows. . . . From the centre of the room dangled some wires, attached to which was a single, naked, electric bulb" (223).

Mah intertwines Niang's mixed heritage and her control over money in a move that reinforces the link between desire for the West and narcissistic, capitalist excess. She further emphasizes Niang's privilege and mobility when Niang declares in 1997, "Your father and I are really citizens of the world. If the situation looks bad, we can fly to any country at a moment's notice" (233). Mah thus juxtaposes two models of femininity here: the global capitalist "Eurasian" with flexible citizenship, and the maternal citizen who is inextricably bound to nation. In this paradigm, the global capitalist personifies upheaval, loss of identity, and the disintegration of the nuclear family; and her contrast of Niang and Aunt Baba calls forth two visions of Chinese peoples in the twentieth century—one in which the Chinese diaspora, spurred by money and consumption, abandons family and homeland for the West, and the other in which those in China are subject to persecution, deprivation, and separation from the West.

The gendered opposition between excess/hybridity and deficiency/purity reinforces the notion of women as caretakers of home, family, and national tradition. And yet, even as Mah defines ideal femininity as located within China and defined by sacrifice and trauma, the uneven distribution of capital does not in and of itself signal the denial of family and nation. Instead, Mah argues that acceptable forms of economic success can also be a marker of women's resistance to traditional gender roles. Mah's journey from unwanted daughter to enlightened doctor is largely propelled by the mothers, grandmothers, and great-aunts that precede her, and much of her story revolves around women who have rejected traditional definitions of womanhood in China. Mah's great aunt—purported lesbian and owner of the first women's bank in China—marks the beginning of Mah's narrative. She writes, "At the age of three my great aunt proclaimed her independence by categorically refusing to have her feet bound, resolutely tearing off the bandages as fast as they were applied" (5). Mah's beginning calls forth many U.S. readers' assumptions regarding the oppressed status of women in China, even as she begins with her great aunt's rejection of that positioning. She adds:

> In 1924 Grand Aunt founded her own bank, the Shanghai Women's Bank. . . . Her bank was staffed entirely by women and designed to meet their specific needs. In they came: spinster daughters, with their inheritance and nest eggs;

> first wives (called big wives), with their dowries and winnings from mah-jong; concubines (called little wives). With cash presents from their men; and professional and educated women, who were tired of being patronized at male-dominated establishments. Shanghai Women's Bank was profitable from the very beginning and remained so until Grand Aunt's resignation in 1953. (9)

Here women's resistance against the larger structures of patriarchy are rendered particularly visible through popular symbols of Chinese women's oppression—bound feet, polygamy, and concubines. While it is easy to read these symbols as highly charged ones in the narrative of resistance against "Eastern" patriarchy, what's important is Mah's linking of "feminism" to Grand Aunt's and other women's circulation and accumulation of money. Unlike Niang's excessive consumption of French and Chinese products, and Aunt Baba's dispossession, Grand Aunt personifies the ideal rate of accumulation, one that succeeds in establishing feminist resistance as an important moment ("in 1924") in Chinese history. The model vision of Chinese femininity thus is recast using quintessential American rhetoric (Grand Aunt "proclaimed her independence") and solidly connects her feminist refusal to have her feet bound and her entry into history's records with her savvy business acumen.

Grand Aunt's business success is echoed by Mah's own economic triumph as she becomes an anesthesiologist in the United States. She recalls her father's pleasure during his first visit to her home in California. "Our housekeeper Ginger opened the front door when we arrived. Framed against the backdrop of tall bamboos in the airy atrium were our two children, Roger and Ann, running eagerly towards us to greet their grandparents. Father crossed the threshold, stopped and gave a small gasp of pleasure at the glorious view of the harbour from our doorway through the soaring, bright, plant-laden foyer" (213). Mah manages to achieve a combination of Niang's wealth and Aunt Baba's focus on family. Her professional achievements in the United States effect the ultimate transcendence of the borders of time and space that have seemed so restricting in the memoir; and in California she is able to momentarily create the ideal version of family. Mah embodies quintessential Chinese womanhood. Distant from the current elaborations of nation and Chinese patriarchy, she is free to locate her economic successes in the West (the only site in which such an elaboration is presumably currently possible), where capitalism can thus be featured as evolving at exactly the right pace, at neither the hyperspeed of Hong Kong or dismantled by the poverty of Communist China. Here she reassures readers that a controlled and continuous accumulation of capital is the means for familial and national unity. That this is a memoir of an "unwanted Chinese daughter," suggests that want, alienation, trauma, and rejection of the Chinese woman can be ultimately transformed into her acceptance, nurturance, satisfaction, and economic success. The predictable trajectory of her work also defines Chinese history's inevitability alongside capitalism's reliability and positions Chinese women as the ideal means of ensuring the steady progress of both.

These interdependent narratives of China and Chinese women in the twentieth century set the stage for the narrative's final reconciliation between Adeline and Aunt Baba, and on a larger scale, an imagined future reunion of the Chinese diaspora, China, and the West. Even as we have entered a phase in which national borders can no longer contain the flows of capital, culture, and peoples, nations themselves—especially China—continue to serve as specters of the global future. As Aunt Baba herself promises, "The way I see it the nineteenth century was a British century. The twentieth century is an American century. I predict that the twenty-first century will be a Chinese century. The pendulum of history will swing from the *ying* ashes brought by the Cultural Revolution to the *yang* phoenix arising from its wreckage" (226). China thus serves simultaneously as an imagined past and an imagined future for the West, one that documents the mass upheavals and traumas of the twentieth century and at the same time promises a future site for global development and economic profit.

History as Modernity

The logic of economic exchange also grounds May-lee and Winberg Chai's *The Girl from Purple Mountain*. Like Mah's *Falling Leaves*, the father-daughter memoir deploys scenes of mass upheaval as a means to highlight the endurance and empowerment of Chinese women, as well as to position Chinese women as emblematic of the modern and epic sweep of history. In a passage that echoes the rhetoric of *Falling Leaves*, May-lee Chai notes:

> [My grandparents] witnessed the fall of the Qing dynasty and the birth of the Republic of China. They then saw the promise of democracy dashed as their country disintegrated into regions controlled by warlords. They survived the Japanese invasion of China, fleeing the Rape of Nanjing in 1937, moving from city to city, one step ahead of the Japanese army. After the Communists won the civil war, they fled to Taiwan then finally immigrated to New York in 1955. (9–10)

The rise-and-fall, to-and-fro movement here is reinforced by the multiple perspectives from which the story is told. Alternating sections, May-lee Chai and her father Winberg Chai attempt to unravel the life of Winberg's mother, and May-lee's grandmother, Ruth Mei-en Chai, and in so doing effect a sweep across generations and continents, moving back and forth from present to past, and from the United States to China.

May-lee and Winberg Chai's efforts to excavate Ruth's story suggests that wholeness can be achieved by reconciling these oppositions in time and space. Winberg explains, "It is my duty to try to understand my mother, to seek answers. To ignore the past is too much like forgetting. And to forget the past would be to dishonor my parents" (7). May-lee echoes her father's emphasis on the importance of piecing together the past. She questions her lack of knowledge beyond the "official story" she has been told. She writes, "But nothing in the official version of the story of their lives helped me to understand my grandmother" (11). And she admits, "I despaired of ever understanding anything" (19). The question of "understanding," of making coherent what seems insensible, becomes a crucial element of these memoirs. The chaos of early twentieth-century China serves as a backdrop against which knowledge of oneself can be achieved. Leslie Bow notes a similar phenomenon that occurs in Amy Tan's *The Joy Luck Club*. Bow writes, "China is portrayed as the location of woman's suffering and America embodies the opportunity for women's choices. Based on this dichotomy, ethnic consciousness is achievable through the following: until the daughters accept their Chinese mothers' lessons about womanhood, they will not understand what it means to be Chinese" ("Cultural Conflict/Feminist Revolution in Amy Tan's *The Joy Luck Club*," 241). While this is also true to some extent of these tributes to Chinese women's triumph over twentieth-century Chinese history, what is also working in these texts is the way that women's embodiment of history—and modernity—operates to enlighten their Chinese American descendants and their Western readers. While their suffering does indeed enable Chinese American women's ethnic and feminist consciousness, as my reading of Pang-mei Natasha Chang's *Bound Feet* will demonstrate, it also renders Chinese women as synonymous with twentieth-century upheaval; to use Bow's formulation, until U.S. readers accept the trauma of twentieth-century Chinese womanhood, they will not understand what it means to be a global citizen.

The Girl from Purple Mountain, like *Falling Leaves*, is equally concerned with loss—not the loss of money but the loss of property, and once again the figure of Chinese woman is posited as the primary means by which property can be recovered and secured. Evoking pre–eighteenth-century European laws of land ownership,[3] by which property was primarily transferred through inheritance rather than through sale, the Chais repeatedly write of Ruth's efforts to maintain and reclaim her mother's property, her own son, her possessions, and her house. Ruth here works against the transfer of ownership of property, a circulation that has been made unpredictable by Japanese imperialism, widespread thievery, and, as the Chais seem to suggest, the emotional and impulsive actions of men. Ruth Mei-en Chai often acts to remedy her husband's rash, sometimes generous decisions, a role that enables the contradictory definition of Chinese women as keepers of tradition and nation and as feminist rebels.

When Ruth's mother dies and her father immediately remarries his "personal maid," Ruth vows to "avenge" her death. When her father decides to sell his deceased wife's possessions and property, Ruth sues him. Ruth's son Winberg remembers, "It was a bold move. The laws protecting property were new, the civil law code was revised every few years, and a woman's claim to property was a dicey affair. But . . . [n]o one wanted to be embroiled in a messy lawsuit. No one dared try to buy my grandmother's properties now. My mother's inheritance was safe" (118). Resisting the liquidation of land into monies, and their movement into the public sphere, Ruth maintains the integrity of family (against the image of her father's assumed rejection of her mother) and their ties to nation by retaining family possessions. At the same time, the "boldness" of her legal maneuver identifies her ability to navigate easily the shifting legal and political terrain of the 1930s. Ruth's fight is thus also cast in a feminist light, claiming not only women's empowerment within a legal context but also a sense of sisterhood with wives who are abandoned by their husbands for younger women.

Ruth's own property itself becomes difficult to preserve. When Ruth and her family are forced to flee Nanjing, Japanese army officers commandeer Ruth's home for their own use. When the family returns in 1945, Ruth discovers that the house now serves as a brothel. Although the house has been ruined, Ruth is given credit for recovering and restoring it.

> [M]y mother used my father's connections to procure building supplies and construction crews to repair her dream house. At night when the workmen had gone home, we dug holes in the backyard trying to find the treasures we had buried there. The money we had hidden in the well was gone, but my mother did find the Yi-xing clay tea set her mother had given to her for graduation so long ago. She'd buried it

near the wall and neither the Japanese officers who'd been stationed in our house nor the Russian had found it. (230)

The reoccupation of her home works on two levels: on a nationalist one in that she is able to outlast the Japanese invasion of her home and country; and again at the level of womanhood whereby she rescues the home from being a house of prostitution and thus returns woman to the role of matriarch rather than sex worker. The recovery of prized objects also works to consolidate her position as guardian of tradition and history.

Ruth's ability to recover and preserve property is underscored by her ability to also earn money. Shortly after the renovations are complete, she rents her house to Americans, despite her son's protests. "But my mother explained that we had to be practical. The Americans had money, money that was worth something. . . . She had built a comfortable house, I knew. And they were grateful to live in such a residence; they didn't want to live like Chinese people, filthy and cold, everyone packed together in one room. My mother understood what Americans expected from a house" (231). Winberg Chai here distinguishes between "money" and "money that was worth something." Even as Winberg and Ruth acknowledge that the system undergirding Chinese currency has collapsed, and that American money is "worth something," Ruth's actions become exemplary for her ability to locate and preserve "worth," her capacity to distinguish between value systems and profit from her knowledge of U.S. sensibilities and customs.

Ruth's ability to conserve property and cultural artifacts is constantly demonstrated, for the theme of loss runs heavily through this and other twentieth-century Chinese women's epics. Thievery, in particular, plays a prominent role in the narrative. When Ruth and Charles first return to China, many of their belongings are stolen. Ruth herself battles her sister-in-law for her own clothes and jewelry. When Charles promises his brother that he can adopt Ruth and Charles' newborn son, Ruth is outraged. Winberg remembers, "My mother insisted that we move from my uncle's house. (I mean, my uncle that thief! That scoundrel! That bandit!)" (164). The threat of thieves haunts Winberg himself: "My amah explained all this. Thieves who broke into rich people's houses and slit the sleeping people's throats, even the poor servants, and stole everything inside, including sleeping babies, whom they took away to their mountain hideaways and forced them to act as their servants until they were old enough to become thieves too" (137). Property cannot be secured (especially from the threat of her husband's family), May-lee and Winberg Chai narrate, and its unpredictability becomes part of a larger pattern of chaos and trauma that defines twentieth-century China for Western readers.

The cycle of loss and recovery of material goods stands as metaphor for the same cycle of loss and recovery of family, home, history, tradition, and nation—certainly the sweeping epic nature that constitutes these types of narratives. The property that she repeatedly saves is indeed symbolic of the preservation of Chinese culture itself. Ruth gives her son a stone with a note that reads, "This stone came from Purple Mountain, Outside the Capital of the Republic of China, Nanjing, 1948." Whenever May-lee visits her grandparents in Manhattan, she is allowed to take one of many different types of Chinese objects—cloisonné vases, jade trees, scrolls of paintings. Invariably she chooses a box of stones, the least materially valuable of all of the items but certainly the one that has the most cultural and geographic symbolism. In the global capitalist era in which exchange value can shift in a shorter amount of time and over a larger amount of space, Chinese women emerge as successful negotiators and preservers of value and values.

Ruth's ability to preserve familial, communal, and national history is juxtaposed with numerous descriptions of her as exemplary modern woman. May-lee introduces her, "My grandmother, 'Ruth' Mei-en Tsao, was one of the first women admitted into a national university in China when the government finally allowed women to attend in 1920" (10). Winberg Chai also heralds his mother's unique and singular status. "My mother was the most beautiful woman alive in China. Everyone who knew her would tell you so. She was born into a wealthy family, a good family, an old respectable family from the north" (21). The elite status that Ruth is accorded serves to emphasize even further her abilities to rise above the chaos of the turbulent century, and her successive triumphs and unbreakable will only enable her to take her place in a long of line of women ahead of their time. For example, in a description of Ruth's mother's rebellion against having her own feet bound—a scene strikingly similar to that in Mah's *Falling Leaves* and another in Chang's *Bound Feet and Western Dress*—Winberg writes of his grandmother's reaction, "And in the beginning, my mother's mother cried with lungs that exploded with power, like steam engines. . . . The shrieks continued nonstop for three months, unabated. No one could remember a child with such strength and willpower, especially a girl" (23). The power of Ruth's mother's voice and of Ruth's own beauty and intellect speaks to their refusal to be constrained by the conventional social dictates surrounding women.

As Winberg Chai writes about Ruth, "My mother should have been a man" (35). Such declarations call forth the ultimate transgression and compliment—that she has achieved the social status of men. Simultaneously highlighting the presumed strict demarcations of gender roles in China (that is, that Chinese women possess neither power nor value while Chinese men are oppressive and controlling) and extolling the strength of Ruth Chai in her ability to reverse these positions, May-lee and Winberg Chai highlight the figure of the Chinese woman as straddling boundaries of gender, time, and place. Unlike the Chinese diasporic man with "flexible citizenship," the Chinese diasporic woman does not move across national borders; instead, she evokes the specific characteristics of nation—its history, politics, social structures, and geography—to transcend them. Her refusal to be contained by boundaries and limits of any kind allows U.S. readers to imagine that "authentic" Chinese history—verified by dates and locations—is in fact a universal past, filled with every type of suffering and conversely every kind of triumph.

The collapse of borders is once again emphasized in the authors' conflation of the past and the "modern." Despite their look back in time, the Chinese women who are memorialized in the narratives are not situated in an ancient and forgotten era; instead they are almost always described in terms that establish their embodiment of modernity. Ruth's coming of age parallels the rise of the republic, during which, "the Chinese character for ocean, *yang*, also came to mean 'foreign,' 'Western,' and 'modern'" (55). In describing Ruth's insistence on choosing her own husband, Winberg Chai notes, "These were modern times, not the feudal past; there should only be love marriages, no more arranged marriages" (71). And when Ruth's mother finds out that Ruth will attend graduate school in the United States, she approves: "You can be married in America. . . . A modern woman. Just as you always wanted" (73). The modern consists not only of present events in the United States, but paradoxically can also be found in early twentieth-century China. Cut off from its "natural" progression by the Communist takeover of China in 1949, the potential of "modernity" remains intact within the Chinese woman's body, waiting to be excavated by future Chinese American generations. The abrupt disruption of history is particularly played out in Ruth and Winberg's last visit to their ancestors' graves, before fleeing Nanjing in 1937. At the temple, Ruth promises that Winberg's name and accomplishments will be carved on the polished stone tablets, alongside those of previous generations. Winberg, however, writes, "As it turned out, nothing more would be recorded for our family. The war would scatter us all across China and then across the world, and then in the 1960s, the Red Guards would come and destroy the family temple, smashing the statues and the stone steles, setting fire to the bamboo plaques and the rice-paper books recording the history of the Chai family" (151). The dramatic description of the destruction of "history" counters Ruth's and China's forward trajectory toward the modernity of the West. Instead, history and time itself seem to be interrupted by the invasion and the eventual Communist takeover. The ideological divide between China and the "West" is thus depicted as a break in time, in which neither past nor future exist, only endless and directionless movement. This figuration of twentieth-century China corresponds with Johannes Fabian's argument that the East is often imagined to occupy an earlier temporal position with respect to the West. Often representing the primitive or the ancient, Africa and Asia thus stand as counterparts and "other" to the modern and progressive "West." *The Girl from*

Purple Mountain and other books in this genre remove China from the opposition and instead position it outside of time's continuum.

The opposition between the promise of Ruth's future at the creation of the Republic and the erasure of that future is again emphasized with the destruction of the family home. Built with proceeds from her mother's inheritance (again underscoring matrilineal rather than patrilineal ties), Ruth's house is characterized as "modern": "Not just any house, but the perfect home, the foundation for the rest of her life. Modern. Western. . . . All of my childhood, I'd heard of this miracle house, the best house in the world, my grandmother's modern, American-style brick dream house" (123). When May-lee and Winberg return in 1985, however, the house has fallen into disrepair. In a rundown neighborhood, dotted with "tin-roofed shanties and squatters' shacks . . . we found a long narrow brick house, now sooty-gray and dilapidated, with two brick columns that must have been imposing once but that now seemed merely in need of supports" (123). Upon discovery, Winberg rants, "You've ruined everything! Everything is dirt! Everything is poor! The country is poor! You've ruined China! The Communists have ruined everything!" (123). The juxtaposition between "modern," "American," and "Western" and poverty, dilapidation, and Communism highlights again the narrative's trajectory from cultural and social promise to economic decline. The book closes with another trip to China in which capitalism seems to have taken hold. "Our relatives all had refrigerators and color television sets now. The women were wearing skirts and high heels. My father's cousin . . . had received a visa to work in New York at Columbia University. We celebrated with a seventeen-course banquet" (296). The markers of "success" abound, and the narrative ends where it begins, with the image of a changing China, one that is moving to embrace Western cultural values and capitalism.

"A Woman Is Nothing?"[4]

I turn now to a discussion of Pang-Mei Natasha Chang's *Bound Feet and Western Dress: A Memoir*. I have spent some time making visible Chinese women's seemingly innate abilities to locate, direct, maintain, and recover money and property, but what remains to be examined is the value of Chinese women themselves in what Gayle Rubin has termed the "economics and politics [of] sex/gender systems" (205). Rubin, looking at the kinship systems described by Lévi-Strauss, as well as Freud's theories of gender identification, reveals the social apparatuses that designate women as exchangeable while men retain the power to exchange and the profits of that exchange. She writes, "'Exchange of women' is a shorthand for expressing that the social relations of a kinship system specify that men have certain rights in their female kin, and that women do not have the same rights either to themselves or to their male kin. In this sense, the exchange of women is a profound perception of a system in which women do not have full rights to themselves" (177).

The exchange of women lies at the heart of Chang's *Bound Feet and Western Dress*. Following a format similar to *The Girl from Purple Mountain*, the memoir is told from two perspectives: that of the author, Pang-Mei Natasha Chang, and of her great aunt, Chang Yu-i, the first woman in China to get a divorce. The narrative again juxtaposes two time periods—the beginning and the end of the twentieth century—and two locales—China and the United States—in order to highlight the struggles that each of the women face. Beginning almost each chapter with her own questions about her place in the family's hierarchy and in larger social and national structures, Pang-Mei Natasha Chang then moves back in time to her great aunt's struggles to negotiate family and society. She particularly makes parallels between her own efforts to locate a Chinese American identity and her aunt's negotiations of the cultural changes that characterize early twentieth-century China—the loosening of social restrictions on Chinese women, especially the abandonment of practices such as foot-binding, and the increased interaction between China and Western nations such as the United States and England. Her great aunt's fame as the first woman to get a divorce in China—that is, her notoriety for rejecting the role of wife—becomes the primary means through which Pang-Mei herself is able to locate her own identity in a national and international history that primarily revolves around the accomplishments of men.

The act of writing her great aunt's story presumably serves to disrupt the formal narrative of the Chang family from which Pang-Mei finds herself alienated. She explains the ways in which the men in the Chang family have achieved distinction, and how their public triumphs have been the foci of the Chang family narrative. In the respected realms of politics, economics, science, and education, where her grandfather and great uncles have joined the ranks of elite historymakers as the heads of political parties, banks, and universities, Pang-Mei does not see a place for herself.

> While proud of my grandfather and great-uncles, I did not know to what extent I dared identify with them. These were Chang men. Whenever the family talked about my great-aunts the Chang women, they praised their successful marriage to educated or wealthy men, and their elegant skills in social situations. . . . I worried where that left me, a first-generation Chinese-American girl who had never been to China. (39)

The unacceptability of such a patriarchal narrative and of her own invisibility in its annals is made manifestly clear, and it seems equally apparent that her U.S. readers would reject such a relegation of women to the role of wife and social coordinator. Instead, Pang-Mei looks to her great aunt, Chang Yu-i, as a means of breaking free from such restricting kinship structures. What Chang's narrative contradictorily demonstrates, however, is that the value of Chinese women for not only Pang-Mei but U.S. readers depends on her aunt's ability to maintain and keep intact existing kinship systems, especially during the early part of twentieth-century China—a period that Chang writes, "witnessed tremendous upheavals of traditional Confucian culture as Western ideals pushed to the fore" (5). Despite her great aunt's divorce (initiated entirely by her husband), she continues to fulfill the other roles that kinship demands—dutiful daughter-in-law, doting mother, loving sister. Her ability to maintain these familial ties models for her great nieces the same type of tension found in other works of this genre—the embrace of resistance and modernity against traditional patriarchal values, even as the Chinese women become the vehicle through which home, family, and nation are maintained.

Chinese women's negotiation of the political and social changes of the twentieth century, and their ability to speak to Western audiences, depends entirely on the language of value. The first chapter told in Chang Yu-i's voice is entitled, "A Woman Is Nothing." She tells her great niece, "I am your grandfather's sister, Chang Yu-i, and before I tell you my story, I want you to remember this: in China, a woman is nothing. When she is born, she must obey her father. When she is married, she must obey her husband. And when she is widowed she must obey her son. A woman is nothing, you see. This is the first lesson I want to give you so that you will understand" (6). *Nothingness* here is equated with her status with respect to the men in her family. Chang Yu-i notes here that as an object of exchange—transferred from father to husband to son—she is unable to retain any of the benefits of this circulation.

She makes even more explicit the terms of her exchange by describing the conditions under which the transaction is effected.

> Using his formal name, Chang Chia-ao, fourth Brother suggested a match between Hsü Chih-mo and me. Shortly thereafter, Hsü Chih-mo's father sent a note personally approving the match. Fourth Brother had already begun to earn a reputation in the area and to restore our family name to one of wealth and esteem. Hsü Chih-mo's father wrote very simply: 'I, Hsü Shen would be honored to have Chang Chia-ao's sister.' And that is how Hsü Chih-mo and I became engaged. (67)

Even as she highlights her lack of agency in the transaction as well as the exchange's primary purpose, which is to enhance the status of the men making the transfer, Chang Yu-i nevertheless fetishizes the formal structure of the arrangement. What are the circumstances under which these two impulses—to elaborate on woman as commodity even while upholding the structures that make that devaluation possible—work together to form a narrative that is lauded to be instructive and inspiring to future Chinese American female generations and to U.S. readers generally?

The "nothingness" of womanhood is further emphasized by the divorce itself. The rejection of her husband, a famous poet and intellectual in early twentieth-century China, does not in fact break down the boundaries of kinship that restrict her movement from one male family member to the next. Although Hsü Chih-mo's actions are read as a sign of his denunciation of tradition and Confucian values, the memoir works to render the divorce as further interrogation of Chang Yu-i's fulfillment of her responsibilities. She wonders, "Why a divorce? Did he think that I served him or his family poorly? Did he think that I was unwilling to accept a concubine?" (123). Contrary to her statement that a woman's "nothingness" stems directly from her status as object rather than agent of exchange, Chang Yu-i's primary means of reclaiming that value is through upholding the system itself. Such a strategy is suggested by Hsü Chih-mo himself when he asks if she would be willing to continue on as daughter-in-law even if she is no longer his wife. Despite her claims that the two are interdependent, she ultimately performs that role even after Hsü Chih-mo remarries. Years after the divorce, her mother-in-law, upset over her son's new domestic situation, comes to Chang Yu-i. "'The family has come to ruin,' Lao Taitai said. 'I don't want to live here anymore. Lao Ye and I want to move in with you.' I had never heard Lao Taitai so upset. She had never before said to me that she wanted to transfer her household to mine" (185). Chang Yu-i suggests here the transformations that take place within the kinship system of exchange. By her mother-in-law's transfer of her own household to Chang Yu-i's, she makes visible the dependence of the kinship system's operation on her role. It becomes even further elucidated when Lao Taitai dies, and Hsü Chih-mo begs Chang Yu-i to perform the funeral rites. At the funeral itself, "I took my place next to Hsü Chih-mo . . . as the adopted daughter of the Hsü family" (191). Despite Hsü Chih-mo's rejection of traditional family structures, Chang depicts his actions as born less out of philosophy than out of selfishness, cowardice, and impetuousness. Chang Yu-i emerges instead as the foundation of family and tradition.

Even when she adopts an attitude that resists her role as "wife," she does so by embracing her status as "mother." When Hsü Chih-mo finds out that Chang Yu-i is pregnant with their second child, he tells her to get an abortion. She later tells her great niece, "I made the decision to disobey Hsü Chih-mo for the first time in my life, and to keep my child. . . . If he was going to desert me in such a fashion, why should I be the good wife and obey his request for an abortion? I would not abandon my child in the same abrupt way Hsü Chih-mo had deserted me in Sawton" (130). Even if her husband has abdicated his role in the kinship system, Chang Yu-i has not, and her ensuring that the economics of that system continue to operate smoothly is the basis for the economics of these "Gone with the Wind" memoirs. Like the other texts discussed in this chapter, *Bound Feet and Western Dress* positions Chinese women as the element of stability in a nation threatened by the decline of political and social structures. Through the language and logic of economic exchange, Chang Yu-i and others "resist" their "nothingness" by pointing continuously to the ways in which family, nation, and capital have been enhanced by their contributions.

Chang Yu-i's business success is, not surprisingly, effortless. During the wars against Japan and between the Communist and Nationalist parties, she profits from purchasing large quantities of the dye used to make uniforms and sells it for "one hundred times the price." "With this capital," she tells us, "I started investing in cotton and gold. Of all the people in the dress shop, only I made money, no one else" (202). Vice President of Shanghai Women's Savings Bank,[5] as well as general manager of one of her brother's dress shops, and later treasurer of another brother's political party, "the National Socialist," Chang Yu-i repeatedly highlights her sense of order and responsibility. In 1937 when the bank's collapse seems imminent due to the Japanese invasion, she asks a customer to leave his funds in the bank. He tells her, "If you, Chang Yu-i, tell me that you guarantee it, I believe you. I would not trust anyone else's word, but yours I will trust." She later adds, "We drew up an agreement that I would give him the money in six months with interest. In this way I saved our bank. I carried the guarantee on my person at all times for the next half year. In case anything happened to me, I wanted the people who found me to know my responsibility to this customer" (203). Her business acumen and sense of duty, whether to family or patrons, defines her, like the other Chinese heroines in these narratives, as the seeming epitomes of history and profit.

Her status as standing outside of the traditional structures of kinship (as a divorced woman) and yet enabling the existence of those structures (as aunt, sister, daughter-in-law, and mother) also translates into her straddling of a number of borders: business woman vs. family member, modern vs. traditional, "West" vs. "East." She tells her niece, "You ask me how I could run a bank, a dress shop, and still be so obedient to the Hsüs and Hsü Chih-mo. I thought that I had a duty to the Hsüs because they were my son's grandparents, and therefore my elders. I grew up with these traditional values; I could not discard them, no matter how Western I became" (201). The implicit alignment of China with family and traditional values and the West with business becomes a resonating opposition for U.S. readers. By framing the Chinese woman as the gateway between the private and public spheres, we can see that she becomes the only viable conduit through which the circulation of goods between these two realms is made possible.

This dual responsibility of enabling circulation within both the private and public realms offers Pang-Mei Natasha Chang a logical means of negotiating her own position within the Chang family. The declared contradiction of her identity as "a first-generation Chinese American girl who had never been to China" is made whole through her aunt's narrative of the circulation of monies and commodities. China is made possible through her own kinship relationship with her aunt, while she simultaneously escapes being located solely within those relationships, and by extension being defined as a woman who is "nothing." Able to participate in both the domestic spheres inhabited by her mother and aunts as well as the public spheres of her father and uncles, Chang assuages racial alienation and historical and familial placelessness, not by claiming a place within Asian American history, but instead by writing the story of her aunt in early twentieth-century China, a woman who personifies the "in between," who moves across boundaries of gender, nation, and time.

Chang, ironically but inevitably, closes her narrative with the same symbol of the memoir's opening, her great-aunt's cheongsam. She writes:

> I have come now to place two articles of clothing in the trunk alongside Yu-i's. My two wedding dresses. The first, a gown of white chiffon—the stuff of my American childhood fantasies—I wore as I pronounced my marriage vows. The second dress, a full-length silk sheath in bright red, the Chinese color for felicity. Slim, slitted and topped with a stiff, stand-up collar, my cheongsam is modeled after those worn by Yu-i and my mother. When I changed into my cheongsam for my wedding reception, I felt vibrant and proud, at once a filial daughter and self-reliant sister, though I had broken with tradition and married, with my parents' blessings, outside of my heritage. (211–212)

Chang reinstates the kinship system, but seems to suggest that because her exchange is being effected across ethnic and racial boundaries, it is not subject to the same rules of valuing that established her aunt's "nothingness." Although I would argue that Chang merely moves the traffic across racial boundaries, it is important to emphasize again that Chang's racial positioning becomes inextricably tied to her non-traditional-yet-traditional position to marriage. The alternation of wedding dresses suggests movement outside of traditional boundaries, but ultimately, of course, the false opposition of choices only leads to the same outcome: her own marriage, a wedding that accomplishes the same thing as her great-aunt's divorce, the consolidation of kinship systems and a woman's place within those systems, even while positing and proclaiming Chinese and Chinese

American women's independence. Early twentieth-century China thus emerges as a historical time that captures the "traditional" customs of feudal China—rituals that most evoke for a Western audience "the Orient"—while also bringing forth the revolutionary spirit of the era, the birth of the new republic, the new freedoms for women, and increased interaction with the United States and Europe. As a symbol of this new (pre-Communist) nation, Chang Yu-i can be deployed as a quintessential Chinese foremother for contemporary Chinese American women, located within a specific history and geography and yet transcending all boundaries of time and place.

Conclusion

And yet what are the implications of this alignment for Asian Americans? How does turning to China effect a different Chinese American history from a glance backwards at, for example, Chinese immigrant women in San Francisco in the 1930s? The locating of foremothers in China does correspond with the history of Chinese Americans. Due to anti-Asian immigration legislation, Chinese women were restricted from entering the United States; thus as Gary Okihiro points out, many of them were counted on to maintain home and family in China while Chinese American men labored in California. The social realities of the transnational family even in the early twentieth century thus continue to support arguments for locating Asian American history outside of U.S. borders. At the same time, however, *Bound Feet and Western Dress*, as well as *Fallen Leaves*, *The Girl from Purple Mountain*, and other narratives like it spurn Asian American history and instead embrace a global "history," in its current postmodern form. They imagine Chinese American women's history not necessarily as a history rooted in the moment of immigration to the United States (even though most eventually conclude in that manner), but instead as one grounded in migration in general, a perpetual state to be inhabited, one that embodies the moment of economic exchange. Unlike their male counterparts, they imagine without ever quite realizing a "flexible cultural citizenship," in which their spectacular strength and determination enable their entry into any nation even as that entry is predicated on their personification of China.

The "flexibility" of their position exists on a primary symbolic level, in their ability to promote, control, and encourage the circulation of money and the preservation of property. Ostensibly about Chinese women's battles throughout the twentieth century against epic forces such as national disasters, foreign invasion, or civil war, the memoirs also repeatedly reiterate Chinese women's history as a battle surrounding capital, and that history's ability to reconstitute the nation and homeland. Whether fighting the gross imbalance of distribution (in *Falling Leaves*), recovering property (in *The Girl from Purple Mountain*), or acting as objects of or agents for the traffic in commodities (in *Bound Feet and Western Dress*), the Chinese women here all identify as the agents of economic exchange as a means of maintaining intact familial and national ties and establishing Chinese women as "feminists" and "modern"—and therefore (one assumes) women who are fully assimilable into Western culture. While the proliferation of such texts seem to speak to China's continued function as a site for U.S. fantasies about exotic and foreign lands, the narratives also reveal the role of Chinese women's history as a means of negotiating a global capitalist present. Chinese women in these narratives become a means by which to imagine modernity's potential; straddling the boundaries of gender, hemisphere, and time, they stand forever poised on the cusp of the modern era, the realization of which is perpetually deferred by the dramatic events that threaten to overwhelm them. Chinese women's history thus functions as both a marker for the epic past as well as the potential for transformation and realization of a mutually prosperous future. Through them, we simultaneously witness our past and our future, the reassurances of our triumph over war and natural disasters, and the expansive possibilities of global capitalism. Chinese women's history, written also as the history of Chinese American women, becomes global history, not grounded in the United States or in U.S. relations with China, but instead in the disjointed time and space of capitalism's future.

Notes

Introduction

1. Antonio Callari writes, "The economists' homogenous field of goods underlies all constructions of the economy and of the market as a mechanism and can therefore be thought of as the epistemological condition of economics" (253).

2. Jack Amariglio notes, "There is nothing at all 'certain' about any act of exchange, and nothing in it less symbolic or less 'about' power, responsibility, meaning, and so forth. Likewise, there is something fundamentally 'constituted' and 'constituting' about identities and subjectivities in every act of exchange" (269).

3. See Lowe, *Immigrant Acts: On Asian American Cultural Politics*; Palumbo-Liu, *Asian/American: Historical Crossings of a Racial Frontier*; Chuh and Shimakawa, Nguyen, and Chen.

4. As George Lipsitz has written, "Scholars specializing in the study of race and ethnicity have been producing significant new works every year. Ethnic studies programs and departments are proliferating at an accelerated pace. At every level of instruction, lesson plans and curricula reflect an unprecedented attention to issues of identity and power. Yet while Ethnic studies is doing very well, ethnic people are fairing very badly" ("To Tell the Truth and Not Get Trapped," 296).

5. I am indebted to Robert Lee's *Orientals: Asian Americans in Popular Culture* for tracing the history of Asian American identity construction, especially with respect to economic anxieties.

6. Lee notes that after protests from the Japanese Association of South California, the "Japanese" merchant became ethnically identified as Burmese (123).

7. Lee cites striking figures published by the Committee against Anti-Asian Violence, which noted that between 1985 and 1990, hate crimes in New York City rose 680 percent (217); see also *CAAV Voice, Newsletter of the Committee Against Anti-Asian Violence* 2, no. 1 (Spring 1991): 1–2.

8. Lee writes, "In the contemporary labor market, globalized capital is the new yellow peril that threatens to reduce the American worker to the wage levels of Third World workers. The new identification of capital with foreign cultures, from the Indonesian banking conglomerates to the Korean greengrocer, enables the U.S. to camouflage its own leading role in the reorganization of a globalized capitalist economy. The Oriental is, once again, constructed as the alien agent" (223).

9. Fraser writes, "We can no longer assume that the bourgeois conception of the public sphere was simply an unrealized utopian ideal; it was also a masculinist ideological notion that functioned to legitimate an emergent form of class rule" (116).

10. hooks writes, "Currently, the commodification of difference promotes paradigms of consumption wherein whatever difference the Other inhabits is eradicated, *via* exchange, by a consumer cannibalism that not only displaces the Other but denies the significance of that Other's history through a process of decontextualization" (351).

11. For further discussions exploring how race functions as a means of property see Cheryl Harris, George Lipsitz, and Amy Robinson.

12. Janet Sorenson's "'I Talk to Everbody in Their Own Way': Defoe's Economies of Identity" is a particularly useful example of such methodology.

13. Tomo Hattori has also noted the possibilities of deploying Jean-Joseph Goux's theories toward an analysis of Asian American literature. Hattori names "race" as the general equivalent, "as the standard measure that makes human bodies and racial culture commensurable and equal to each other" (230). He contends that the critic who compares Edith Maud Eaton to her sister Winnifred Eaton (usually speaking more favorable of Edith) "exposes the capitalist project of equivalence. A life devoted to truth and justice cannot be declared more true than a life devoted to wealth and fame unless one concedes that the former is measurable in the same terms as the latter" (230).

14. See also Gaytri Chakravorty Spivak's work in *In Other Worlds* and "Poststructuralism, Marginality, Postcoloniality and Value" for a discussion of how economic and social value is and is not connected. Spivak cautions, "We cannot grasp values as such; it is a possibility for grasping, without content. But if we position ourselves *as identities* in terms of links in the chain of a value-coding as if they were persons and things, and go on to ground our practice on

that positioning, we become part of the problem in the ways I am describing." ("Postructuralism, Marginality," 227). My book in essence interrogates how writers of color and critics of race studies locate themselves on that "chain of value-coding," and how that language of and anxiety surrounding equivalence dominates both the logic of social equality as well as the economic routes found in the texts themselves.

15. See Sau-ling Wong, "Denationalization Reconsidered."

16. In fact, the mass consumption of any type of cultural object has generally been regarded as suspect, a sign of upward class mobility or a means of marking class distinction. Although critics have argued that consumption can offer a means of resistance, through the conscious subversive reinterpretation of what the manufacturer or advertiser intended, most critics have pointed to, as Juliet B. Schor and Douglas B. Holt have summarized, the role that consumption plays in consolidating hegemonic narratives of race, class, gender, and sexuality. They explain that critiques of mass consumption have been diverse, ranging from arguments that it reinforces class divisions, has had a devastating impact on a wide range of ecological systems, supports the dominance and restriction of women, stands in opposition to any valid notion of the "aesthetic," and flattens global diversity while relying upon the exploitation of workers on a global scale.

17. Maira, 358. Maira cogently argues that it is precisely the "indigestible" labor of working- and lower middle-class South Asian Americans that consumption of henna and other Indo-chic products elides. She also makes clear that the sudden popularity of Indo-chic products can be linked to anti–South Asian violence, and brings together the cultural and political erasure of South Asian American peoples—both from the products themselves and from U.S. neighborhoods.

Chapter 1

1. 1943 also marks the arrival of a new social climate as well: the easing up of restrictions against Chinese immigration to the United States and the enabling of Chinese immigrants to become naturalized as U.S. citizens. The embrace of China as an ally during World War II, as well as anti-Japanese sentiment, helped to reshape U.S. attitudes toward Chinese Americans and prompted the repeal of the Chinese Exclusion Act, in effect since 1882. While the 1943 repeal did not translate into a flood of Chinese immigration into the United States—a quota of only 105 Chinese people were allowed entry—it did allow the admission of alien Chinese wives of American citizens, an action that had considerable impact on the establishment of Chinese American families in Chinatown and the nation at large. The period between 1943 and 1965 (when the Immigration Act of 1965 abolished the earlier restrictive quotas for Asian immigration) was thus a time

in which Chinese American identity and community became more established in terms of their growing populations and their visibility to the nation at large as a site on which growing anxiety about communist China might be worked out. Paradoxically, even as fear of anticommunist attacks caused left-wing Chinatown authors to destroy their work (see Jinqi Ling [56]" for a lengthier discussion of the political climate surrounding Chinese American writers during that era), a striking number of memoirs and novels by Chinatown writers made their way into major publishing houses and onto bestseller lists.

2. Jinqi Ling also notes the publication of Hazel Lin's *The Physicians* (John Day, 1951), Eileen Chang's *The Rice Sprout Song* (1955); and Diana Chang's *Frontiers of Love* (1956) as also belonging to this genre and published by major mainstream presses (Ling, 56).

Chapter 2

1. "What I am arguing here is that the loosely held and fluctuating collectivity called 'Asian Americans' will dissolve back into its descent-defined constituents as soon as one leaves American national borders behind" (Sau-ling Wong, "Denationalization Reconsidered," 17).

2. New Il-Han's *When I Was a Boy in Korea*, Etsu Sugimoto's *A Daughter of the Samurai*, and Lin Yutang's *My Country and My People* are only a few of the examples Kim provides that attempt "to bridge the gap between East and West" (Kim, *Asian American Literature*, 24).

3. See Gregory L. Ulmer's "The Object of Post-Criticism" for a more complete discussion of collage.

Chapter 3

1. United States Bureau of Citizenship and Immigration Services. "International Matchmaking Organizations: A Report to Congress," February 1999. (http://uscis.gov/graphics/aboutus/repsstudies/Mobrept.htm.) Roland Tolentino puts the numbers of mail-order brides much higher, estimating that 50,000 mail-order brides have emigrated from the Philippines alone in the last decade. It is not clear how he arrived at those estimates.

2. Although the numbers of mail-order brides coming from the former Soviet Union are on the rise, this chapter is primarily concerned with the rhetoric surrounding Asian mail-order brides, particularly those from the Philippines (which have constituted the largest percentage of women listed by international matchmaking organizations from Asia) and Thailand. Web sites list women from countries as varied as the Philippines, Thailand, China, Malaysia, and Japan, and my use of the term *Asian* (although primarily referring to Southeast Asia) is not intended to collapse differences among different Asian nations

but instead to point to the uniformity of descriptions and the lack of differentiation in the media coverage and Web sites themselves.

3. See essays by Rona Tamiko Halualani, Tracey Lai, Roland Tolentino, and Venny Villapando.

4. See Pierrette Hondagneu-Sotelo, 55–69, as well as other essays in the anthology by Arlie Russell Hochschild, Susan Cheever, Rhacel Salazar Parreñas, and Barbara Ehrenreich.

5. Although the numbers of mail-order brides from Eastern Europe are significantly increasing, the rhetoric surrounding their move to the United States differs from the one defining Asian mail-order brides, who are seen as more greedy, disadvantaged, and in need of rescue. Robert Scholes also notes that Asian mail-order brides are substantially younger in age than those coming from the former Soviet Union (Scholes, Appendix A, in "International Matchmaking Organizations").

6. Critics of globalization and its effects on third-world women note that in the current transnational era, Asian women's bodies have been identified as particularly suitable for assembly and manufacturing work because of their imagined "natural" dexterity, small hands, sharp eyes, and general inexperience. See Aihwa >Ong's "The Gender and Labor Politics of Postmodernity" for a discussion of this phenomenon.

7. In an exploration of value and identity, Gayatri Chakravorty Spivak explains the inherent connection between all languages of value, and the futility of determining the first moment of definition: "Thus 'value'. . . must necessarily *also* mean its 'ordinary' language meanings: material worth as well as idealist values, and create the productive confusion that can, alone, give use to practice" (author's italics). See "Poststructuralism, Marginality, Postcoloniality and Value," 242, fn. 20.

8. The 1999 report to Congress on international matchmaking organizations cites figures from the Global Survival Network and Robert Scholes, both of which estimate the numbers of organizations to be around two hundred.

9. www.ajapaneseprincess.com/gen/faq/html

10. www.blossoms.com/asianTours.html

Chapter 4

1. Sau-ling Wong has dubbed these narratives "Gone with the Wind" epics. Wong elaborates, "Virtually all involve a multigenerational family saga interwoven with violent historical events . . . as well as a culminating personal odyssey across the ocean to the West, signaling final 'arrival' in both a physical and ideological sense" (Wong, "Sugar Sisterhood," 200). Wong's use of the phrase "Gone with the Wind" is gleaned from a reviewer's praise of Linda Ching Sledge's *Empire of Heaven*; some of the authors that Wong lists as participating in this

genre include Bette Bao Lord, Nien Cheng, C. Y. Lee, Linda Ching Sledge, Jung Chang, and Lillian Lee. Alice Cairns points specifically to first-person accounts of the Cultural Revolution such as Anchee Min's *Red Azaleas*, Jan Wong's *Red China Blues*, Rae Yang's *Spider Eaters*, and Ting-xing Ye's *A Leaf in the Bitter Wind*. "The essential ingredients are the same. These are true stories, in which the main character/author is an attractive, intelligent woman, struggling to stay morally superior in the political chaos of China. She is usually aided or inspired by a granny with bound feet, a noble mother or an angelic daughter, and held back by a hopeless and/or brutal father. Add to that several hundred screaming Red Guards, the denunciations of once-loyal neighbours and friends, and an uplifting final chapter set in the Free World, and you have the makings of a money-spinner."

2. See also Spivak, *In Other Worlds*, 90.

3. I was greatly assisted in the reading of property in this text by James Thompson's *Models of Value: Eighteenth-Century Political Economy and the Novel*, especially the chapter entitled, "Fielding and Property."

4. Thanks to Matthew Tinkcom for the suggestion for this subtitle.

5. This ironically appears to be the same bank that Adeline Mah's great aunt founds in *Falling Leaves*. Chang Yu-i tells us, "The people who ran the bank before me had given away all the money to friends, relatives, or anyone who asked, and now the bank was almost penniless" (179).

References

Amariglio, Jack. "Give the Ghost a Chance! A Comrade's Shadowy Addendum." In *The Question of the Gift: Essays Across Disciplines*, edited by Mark Osteen, 266–279. London: Routledge, 2002.

Appadurai, Arjun. *Modernity at Large: Cultural Dimensions of Globalization.* Public Worlds 1. Minneapolis: University of Minnesota Press, 1996.

———. *The Social Life of Things: Commodities in Cultural Perspective.* New York: Cambridge University Press, 1986.

Austin, Regina. "'A Nation of Thieves': Consumption, Commerce, and the Black Public Sphere." In *The Black Public Sphere*, 229–252. The Black Public Sphere Collective. Chicago: University of Chicago Press, 1995.

Bow, Leslie. *Betrayal and Other Acts of Subversion: Feminism, Sexual Politics, Asian American Women's Literature*. Princeton, NJ: Princeton University Press, 2001.

———. "Cultural Conflict/Feminist Resolution in Amy Tan's *The Joy Luck Club*." In *New Visions in Asian American Studies: Diversity, Community, Power*, 235–247. Franklin Ng. Association for Asian American Studies Series. Pullman, WA: Washington State University Press, 1994.

Cairns, Alice. "Birds of a Feather." *South China Morning Post*, August 10, 1997, Sunday Magazine, sec. 16. http://www.lexis-nexis.com.

Callari, Antonio. "The Ghost of the Gift: The Unlikelihood of Economics." In *The Question of the Gift: Essays Across Disciplines*, edited by Mark Osteen, 248–265. London: Routledge, 2002.

Chai, May-lee and Winberg Chai. *The Girl from Purple Mountain: Love, Honor,*

War, and One Family's Journey from China to America. 1st ed. New York: Thomas Dunne Books, 2001.

Chang, Andrew. "Love By Mail: As In All Matters of the Heart, More Than a Simple Exchange." ABCnews.com. http://abcnews.go.com/sections/world/DailyNews/mailorder020523.html (May 23, 2002).

Chang, Jung. *Wild Swans: Three Daughters of China*. New York: Simon & Schuster, 1991.

Chang, Pang-Mei Natasha. *Bound Feet and Western Dress: A Memoir*. 1st ed. New York: Doubleday, 1996.

Chin, Frank, Jeffery Paul Chan, Lawson Fusao Inada, and Shawn Wong, eds. *Aiiieeeee!: An Anthology of Asian-American Writers*. Washington, D.C.: Howard University Press, 1983.

Chow, Rey. "Violence in the Other Country: China as Crisis, Spectacle, and Woman." In *Third World Women and the Politics of Feminism*, edited by Chandra Mohanty, Ann Russo, and Lourdes Torres, 81–100. Bloomington: Indiana University Press, 1991.

Chuh, Kandice. *Imagine Otherwise: On Asian Americanist Critique*. Durham: Duke University Press, 2003.

Chuh, Kandice and Karen Shimakawa, eds. *Orientations: Mapping Studies in the Asian Diaspora*. Durham, NC: Duke University Press, 2001.

Constable, Nicole. *Romance on a Global Stage: Penpals, Virtual Ethnography, and "Mail Order" Marriages*. Berkeley, CA: University of California Press, 2003.

Daniels, Roger. *Asian America: Chinese and Japanese in the United States since 1850*. Seattle: University of Washington Press, 1988.

Ehrenreich, Barbara and Arlie Russell Hochschild, eds. *Global Woman: Nannies, Maids, and Sex Workers in the New Economy*. New York: Metropolitan Books, 2003.

Fabian, Johannes. *Time and the Other: How Anthropology Makes Its Object*. New York: Columbia University Press, 1983.

Fraser, Nancy. "Rethinking the Public Sphere: A Contribution to the Critique of Actually Existing Democracy." In *Habermas and the Public Sphere*, edited by Craig Calhoun, 109–142. Cambridge, Massachusetts: MIT Press, 1992.

Goux, Jean-Joseph. "Cash, Check, or Charge?" In *The New Economic Criticism: Studies at the Interface of Literature and Economics (Economics as Social Theory)*, edited by Martha Woodmansee and Mark Osteen, 114–128. New York: Routledge, 1999.

———. *Symbolic Economies: After Marx and Freud*. Translated by Jennifer Curtiss Gage. Ithaca, NY: Cornell University Press, 1990.

Habermas, Jürgen. *The Structural Transformation of the Public Sphere: An Inquiry into a Category of Bourgeois Society*. Translated by Thomas

Burger with Frederick Lawrence. Cambridge: MIT Press, 1989. Originally Published as *Strukturwandel der Öffentlichkeit*. Neuwied, Germany: Luchterhand, 1962.

Hagedorn, Jessica Tarahata, ed. *Charlie Chan Is Dead: An Anthology of Contemporary Asian American Fiction*. New York: Penguin Books, 1993.

Halualani, Rona Tamiko. "The Intersecting Hegemonic Discourses of an Asian Mail-Order Bride Catalog: Filipina 'Oriental Butterfly' Dolls for Sale." *Women's Studies in Communication* 19, no. 1 (1995): 45–64.

Hannerz, Ulf. *Transnational Connections: Culture, People, Places. Comedia*. London and New York: Routledge, 1996.

Harris, Cheryl I. "Whiteness as Property." Harvard Law Review 106, no.8. (June 1993): 1707–1792.

Hattori, Tomo. "Model Minority Discourse and Asian American Jouis-Sense." *Differences: A Journal of Feminist Cultural Studies* 11, no. 2 (1999): 228–247.

Henderson, Diedtra. "Mail-Order Brides: Industry Thrives." *The Seattle Times*, March 4, 1995, final edition. http://www.lexis-nexis.com.

Hondagneu-Sotelo, Pierrette. "Blowups and Other Unhappy Endings." In *Global Woman: Nannies, Maids, and Sex Workers in the New Economy*, edited by Barbara Ehrenreich and Arlie Russell Hochschild, 55–69. New York: Metropolitan Books, 2003.

hooks, bell. *Black Looks: Race and Representation*. Boston, MA: South End Press, 1992.

Ivy, Marilyn. "Critical Texts, Mass Artifacts: The Consumption of Knowledge in Postmodern Japan." *South Atlantic Quarterly* 87.3 (1988): 419–444.

Joseph, Miranda. *Against the Romance of Community*. Minneapolis: University of Minnesota Press, 2002.

Joseph, Raymond A. "Wanted in U.S.: Mail-Order Brides." *Philadelphia Inquirer*, February 5, 1984.

Kang, Laura Hyun Yi. *Compositional Subjects: Enfiguring Asian/American Women*. Durham, NC: Duke University Press, 2002.

Kim, Elaine H. *Asian American Literature: An Introduction to the Writings and Their Social Context*. Philadelphia: Temple University Press, 1982.

———, preface to *Charlie Chan Is Dead: An Anthology of Contemporary Asian American Fiction*, edited by Jessica Hagedorn, xvii–xiv. New York: Penguin Books, 1993.

———, foreword to *Reading the Literatures of Asian America*, edited by Shirley Geok-lin Lim and Amy Ling, xi–xvii. Philadelphia: Temple University Press, 1992.

Koepp, Stephen. "For Sale: America." *Time Magazine*, September 14, 1987. http://www.time.com/time/magazine/article/0,9171,965428,00.html.

Krist, Gary. "The Great Leap Backward." Review of *The Girl From Purple Mountain: Love, Honor, War, and One Family's Journey From China to America*, by May-lee Chai and Winberg Chai. *New York Times*, July 8, 2001, late ed, sec. 7:6. http://www.lexis-nexis.com.

Lai, Tracey. "Asian American Women: Not For Sale." In *Race, Class, and Gender: An Anthology*, edited by Margaret L. Anderson and Patricia Hill Collins, 163–171. Belmont, CA: Wadsworth, 1992.

Landers, Ann. "Women Should Stay in Their Place or They'll Stay Single." *Philadelphia Inquirer*, November 14, 1989.

Larsen, Wanwadee. *Confessions of a Mail-Order Bride: American Life through Thai Eyes*. Far Hills, NJ: New Horizon Press, 1989.

Lee, C. Y. *The Flower Drum Song*. New York: Farrar, 1957.

Lee, Robert G. *Orientals: Asian Americans in Popular Culture.* Asian American History and Culture. Philadelphia: Temple University Press, 1999.

Lee, Virginia. *The House That Tai Ming Built*. New York: Macmillan, 1963.

Li, David Leiwei. "The Production of Chinese American Tradition: Displacing American Orientalist Discourse." In *Reading the Literatures of Asian America*, edited by Shirley-Geok-lin Lim, 319–332. Asian American History and Culture. Philadelphia: Temple University Press, 1992.

Lim, Shirley and Amy Ling, eds. *Reading the Literatures of Asian America.* Asian American History and Culture. Philadelphia: Temple University Press, 1992.

Ling, Jinqi. *Narrating Nationalisms: Ideology and Form in Asian American Literature*. New York: Oxford University Press, 1998.

Lipsitz, George. "'To Tell the Truth and Not Get Trapped': Why Interethnic Antiracism Matters Now." In *Orientations: Mapping Studies in the Asian Diaspora*, edited by Kandice Chuh and Karen Shimakawa, 296–310. Durham, NC: Duke University Press, 2001.

———. *The Possessive Investment in Whiteness: How White People Profit from Identity Politics*. Philadelphia: Temple University Press, 1998.

Lowe, Lisa. *Immigrant Acts: On Asian American Cultural Politics*. Durham, NC: Duke University Press, 1996.

Lowe, Pardee. *Father and Glorious Descendant*. Boston: Little, Brown and Company, 1943.

Mah, Adeline Yen. *Falling Leaves: The True Story of an Unwanted Chinese Daughter*. New York: Broadway Books, 1999.

Maira, Sunaina. "Henna and Hip Hop: The Politics of Cultural Production and the Work of Cultural Studies." *Journal of Asian American Studies* 3, no. 3 (October 2000): 329–369.

Marx, Karl. *Capital: A Critique of Political Economy*. Translated by Ben Fowkes. New York: Vintage Books, 1977.

Mauss, Marcel. *The Gift: The Form and Reason for Exchange in Archaic Societies*. New York: W. W. Norton, 1990.

Minatoya, Lydia. *Talking to High Monks in the Snow: An Asian American Odyssey*. New York: HarperPerennial Edition, 1993.

Miyoshi, Masao. *Off Center: Power and Culture Relations Between Japan and the United States*. Cambridge: Harvard University Press, 1991.

Mura, David. *Turning Japanese: Memoirs of a Sansei*. New York: Atlantic Monthly Press, 1991.

Nguyen, Viet Thanh. *Race and Resistance: Literature and Politics in Asian America*. Oxford, England, and New York: Oxford University Press, 2002.

Nguyen, Viet Thanh and Tina Chen. "Editor's Introduction." *Jouvert: A Journal of Postcolonial Studies*, Spring/Summer 2000. http://social.chass.ncsu.edu/jouvert/v4i3/con43.htm.

Odo, Franklin, preface to *Roots: An Asian American Reader*, edited by Amy Tachiki, Eddie Wong, Franklin Odo, and Buck Wong, vii–xi. Los Angeles: The Regents of the University of California, UCLA Asian American Studies Center, 1971.

Okihiro, Gary Y. *Margins and Mainstreams: Asians in American History and Culture*. Seattle: University of Washington Press, 1994.

Ong, Aihwa. *Flexible Citizenship: The Cultural Logics of Transnationality*. Durham, NC: Duke University Press, 1999.

———. "The Gender and Labor Politics of Postmodernity." In *The Politics of Culture in the Shadow of Capital*, edited by Lisa Lowe and David Lloyd, 61–97. Durham, NC: Duke University Press, 1997.

Osteen, Mark and Martha Woodmansee, eds. "Taking Account of the New Economic Criticism: An Historical Introduction." In *The New Economic Criticism: Studies at the Intersection of Literature and Economics*, 3–50. New York: Routledge, 1999.

Palumbo-Liu, David. *Asian/American: Historical Crossings of a Racial Frontier*. Stanford, CA: Stanford University Press, 1999.

Parry, Jonathan and Maurice Bloch, eds. introduction to *Money and the Morality of Exchange*. Cambridge: Cambridge University Press, 1989.

Reed, Naomi C. "The Specter of Wall Street: 'Bartleby, the Scrivener' and the Language of Commodities." *American Literature* 76, no. 2 (June 2004): 247–273.

Rivera, Geraldo. "The Geraldo Show." February 15, 1989. Transcript #370.

Robinson, Amy. "Forms of Appearance of Value: Homer Plessy and the Politics of Privacy." In *Performance and Cultural Politics*, edited by Ellin Diamond, 237–261. London: Routledge, 1996.

Rubin, Gayle. "The Traffic of Women: Notes on the Political Economy of Sex." In *Toward an Anthropology of Women*, edited by Rayna R. Reiter, 157–210. New York: Monthly Review Press, 1975.

Scholes, Robert. "Appendix A: International Matchmaking Organizations: A Report to Congress." United States Bureau of Citizenship and Immigration Services. February 1999. http://uscis.gov/graphics/aboutus/repsstudies/Mobrept.htm.

Schor, Julie B. and Douglas B. Holt. "Introduction: Do Americans Consume Too Much?" In *The Consumer Society Reader*, vii–xxiii. New York: The New Press, 2000.

Seven, Richard and Thomas W. Haines. "Gunman Felt Duped By Bride From the Start—Wife Alleged Abuse; He Said She Wanted Money, Green Card." *The Seattle Times*, March 4, 1995, final edition. http://www.lexis-nexis.com.

Shell, Marc. *The Economy of Literature*. Baltimore, MD: Johns Hopkins University Press, 1978.

Shimakawa, Karen. *National Abjection: The Asian American Body Onstage*. Durham, NC: Duke University Press, 2002.

Simmel, George. *The Philosophy of Money*. London: Routledge, 1978.

Sorenson, Janet. "'I Talk to Everybody in Their Own Way': Defoe's Economies of Identity." In *The New Economic Criticism: Studies at the Interface of Literature and Economics (Economics as Social Theory)*, edited by Martha Woodmansee and Mark Osteen, 75–94. New York: Routledge, 1999.

Spivak, Gayatri Chakravorty. "Can the Subaltern Speak?" In *Marxism and the Interpretation of Culture*, edited by Cary Nelson and Lawrence Grossberg, 271–313. Urbana: University of Illinois Press, 1988.

———. *In Other Worlds: Essays in Cultural Politics*. New York: Methuen, 1987.

———. "Poststructuralism, Marginality, Postcoloniality and Value." In *Literary Theory Today*, edited by Peter Collier and Helga Geyer-Ryan, 219–244. Ithaca: Cornell University Press, 1990.

Tan, Amy. *The Joy Luck Club*. New York: Ivy Books, 1989.

Taylor, Charles. "Modern Social Imaginaries." *Public Culture* 14, no. 1 (2002): 91–124.

Thompson, James. *Models of Value: Eighteenth-Century Political Economy and the Novel*. Durham, NC: Duke University Press, 1996.

Tizon, Alex and Diedtra Henderson. "The World of the Mail-Order Matchmaker—Blackwells Met Via Bellingham Bride Broker." *The Seattle Times*, March 12, 1995, final edition. http://www.lexis-nexis.com.

Tolentino, Roland B. "Bodies, Letters, Catalogs: Filipinas in Transnational Space." *Social Text* 14, no. 3 (1996): 49–76.

Ty, Eleanor and Donald C. Goellnicht, eds., introduction to *Asian North American Identities: Beyond the Hyphen*, 1–14. Bloomington, IN: Indiana University Press, 2004.

Ulmer, George. "The Object of Post Criticism." In *The Anti-Aesthetic: Essays on Postmodern Culture*, edited by Hal Foster, 83–110. Seattle: Bay Press, 1983.

United States Bureau of Citizenship and Immigration Services. "International Matchmaking Organizations: A Report to Congress." February 1999. http://uscis.gov/graphics/aboutus/repsstudies/Mobrept.htm.

Villapando, Venny. "The Business of Selling Mail-Order Brides." In *Making Waves: An Anthology of Writings By and About Asian American Women*, 318–326. Asian Women United of California. Boston: Beacon Press, 1989.

Whitaker, Mark. "The Editor's Desk." *Newsweek*, May 9, 2005.

White, Theodore H. "The Danger from Japan." *New York Times Magazine*, July 28, 1985, final edition. http://www.lexis-nexis.com.

Wong, Jade Snow. *Fifth Chinese Daughter*. Seattle: University of Washington Press, 1989.

———. *Fifth Chinese Daughter*. 1st ed. New York: Harper, 1950.

Wong, Sau-ling Cynthia. "Autobiography as Guided Chinatown Tour?: Maxine Hong Kingston's *The Woman Warrior* and the Chinese American Autobiographical Controversy." In *Maxine Hong Kingston's* The Woman Warrior: *A Casebook*, edited by Sau-ling Cynthia Wong, 29–53. Casebooks in Contemporary Fiction. New York: Oxford University Press, 1999.

———. "Denationalization Reconsidered: Asian American Cultural Criticism at a Theoretical Crossroads." *Amerasia Journal* 21:1&2 (1992): 1–27.

———. "'Sugar Sisterhood': Situating the Amy Tan Phenomenon." In *The Ethnic Canon: Histories, Institutions, and Interventions*, edited by David Palumbo-Liu, 174–210. Minneapolis: University of Minnesota Press, 1995.

———. *Reading Asian American Literature: From Necessity to Extravagance*. Princeton, NJ: Princeton University Press, 1993.

Wong, Shawn, ed. *Asian American Literature: A Brief Introduction and Anthology*. New York: Longman, 1996.

Yúdice, George. "We Are *NOT* the World." *Social Text* 31/32 (1992): 202–216.

Zakeria, Fareed. "What America Needs To Do." *Newsweek*, May 9, 2005.

Index

Christine So is Associate Professor of English at Georgetown University.